Zero Net Energy Case Study Buildings
Volume 2

Written by
Edward Dean, FAIA
    Bernheim + Dean Inc.

Foreword by
Peter Turnbull
    Principal, Commercial
    Buildings, Pacific Gas and
    Electric Company

April 2016

Published in the United States of America 2016
Pacific Gas and Electric Company
San Francisco, California
www.pge.com

ISBN 978-1530353255
Library of Congress Cataloging-in-Publication (CP) Data available upon request.

Graphic Design: Bernheim + Dean Inc.

Photographs by: Jeremy Bittermann, Bruce Damonte, Edward Dean, Kyle Jeffers, Drew Kelly, Amy Snyder, Ted Van der Linden, David Wakely, Chad Ziemendorf.

Energy Performance Graphs & Charts: Edward Dean FAIA, Bernheim + Dean Inc., with Margaret Pigman, Resource Refocus

Cover Photo: View up to one of the roof skylights at the West Berkeley Branch Library, Photo by Kyle Jeffers.

Table of Contents

Foreword

Upon completing Volume 2 of these Zero Net Energy (ZNE) case studies, it's interesting to reflect upon how the market for ZNE has progressed in the 18 months or so since we published Volume 1 in late 2014. The changes have been significant and widespread across multiple areas.

New Policy Initiatives. Just since 2014, we've seen many new policy initiatives at federal, state and local levels that address high performance buildings and ZNE and their important roles in greenhouse gas (GHG) reduction. President Obama issued Executive Order 13693, *Planning for Federal Sustainability in the Next Decade,* in March, 2015: by 2030, it calls for new federal building construction above 5,000 square feet to be "designed to achieve energy net zero" and for significantly higher levels of energy efficiency in existing federal buildings.

Although ZNE policy initiatives in California were explicitly stated as early as 2008 (see the CPUC's *Long Term Energy Efficiency Strategic Plan*), Governor Brown, in his inaugural address in early 2015, raised the bar: he called out aggressive new targets for much higher levels of grid-scale renewable generation together with much higher levels of energy efficiency in all buildings. These proclamations were quickly followed with legislation: SB 350 was signed in October, 2015, codifying the vision and setting specific targets for renewables (up from 33% to 50% by 2030) and building energy efficiency (a "doubling" of efficiency levels).

We have seen other states, including Massachusetts and Rhode Island, establish state-level ZNE initiatives. As of this writing in the Spring, 2016, at least 18 cities across the country have established ZNE districts[1]. Consideration of ZNE is becoming an accepted tenet of building-scale and development-scale planning across the country.

Perceived Cost. A second big change recently is around the perceived cost of ZNE. It's higher, right? Not necessarily. Today, *rapidly* growing numbers of designers are finding ways to achieve ZNE within typical construction budgets for a given building type in a given location. Just as technical feasibility for ZNE in new construction is now generally accepted for the majority of the building stock going forward—not the case just five years ago—we believe that perceptions around cost issues are changing, too. While certain types of high-performance building features do cost more, it is becoming clear that certain higher-cost features can be mostly or fully offset by lower-cost features: for example, a high-performance building shell (more expensive) can reduce the size and capacity of space cooling equipment (less expensive). In other cases, a developer may choose to include premium building performance features at added cost, but may do so deliberately to attract and satisfy a particular type of market demand such that the added cost is an "investment" is fully recovered (and then some) in the form of rent premiums, faster market uptake and reduced vacancy (see Case Study No. 9 in this volume, *Speculative Office Building at 435 Indio Way*).

It will be interesting to revisit these related issues around ZNE cost and ZNE value in the coming years. Our bet is that high performance means high value.

Retrofit Feasibility. Third, we note growing interest in retrofitting existing buildings to ZNE. Not long ago, such projects were thought to be extremely difficult-to-impossible in most cases, and that they would never pencil out financially for those who did pursue them. Yet we note that *four of the five buildings in this Volume 2 are in fact ZNE retrofits* (and five of the eleven buildings in the two volumes combined).

To be sure, there are real feasibility issues with ZNE retrofits and no one claims all buildings can be retrofit to this level. Still, recalling that ZNE is fundamentally a greenhouse gas (GHG)

---

[1] See http://newbuildings.org/sites/default/files/2014_Getting_to_Zero_Update.pdf

reduction strategy, the case for retrofitting becomes stronger as we consider an emerging fact base around the carbon intensity associated with building brand new buildings versus the preservation of existing buildings: preservation of viable existing building shells and foundations, as it turns out, can be a major GHG reduction strategy (mainly from the avoidance of emissions from producing and transporting new steel and concrete).

Each of the four such buildings we have documented in this Volume 2 are fulfilling the missions established by their owners and producing high levels of occupant satisfaction. As with perceptions around technical feasibility and incremental cost, it will be interesting and instructive to observe changing trends around perceptions of ZNE retrofits.

Against this backdrop of rapid change, we must remind ourselves that buildings go up slowly: the time needed to site, plan, permit, design, construct and occupy even a small, simple building is several years; for large, complex projects, it is a decade or more. Yet we are seeing new emphasis across all levels of government for GHG reduction and ZNE in the built environment. We know we can build to ZNE with little or no incremental cost and we know many buildings can (and should!) be retrofit to ZNE. How quickly can we integrate these trends into the existing development stream? How quickly can we embrace and realize the concept that ZNE means better buildings with higher value?

—*Peter Turnbull, Principal, Commercial Buildings, Pacific Gas & Electric Company*

Introduction

The February 2016 issue of *Architect* magazine, a journal published by the American Institute of Architects, closed with a noteworthy editorial on its last page, entitled "Net Zero Enthusiasm". In it, Editor-in-Chief Ned Cramer says

> *"The most significant technical innovation in architecture since the advent of computer-aided design in the 1970s, the net-zero building could positively reshape our way of life, promoting energy independence, reducing drought and carbon emissions, creating jobs. Alas, it has nothing remotely close to the smartphone's penetration (the International Living Future Institute has only certified 21 examples)...So where's the public dialogue, the demand? Why isn't net-zero as familiar in our technology-worshipping culture as the iPhone? Why don't we talk about it with as much awe as the Tesla Model S?"*

This second volume of zero-net-energy (or "net-zero", if you prefer) case study buildings is another installment in such a conversation that is actually happening in this part of the world, and it includes five *awe*-some examples of this new wave of technical innovation in architecture.

Volume 2 of *Zero Net Energy Case Study Buildings*, like *Volume 1*, provides a detailed discussion and analysis of a number of exemplary buildings designed and, so far, performing at zero-net-energy use over the course of a year[1]. As noted in the Foreword, the time between the occupancy of the Volume 1 buildings and that of the Volume 2 buildings, roughly three to seven years, saw advances in building technologies and dissemination of information about successful strategies for ZNE design. The result has been the informed development of the best approaches to the design and construction of ZNE buildings that are meeting practical requirements of reliability and affordability. Five buildings from this next round of ZNE projects are documented in this publication.

Selection of the Case Study Buildings of Volume 2

In order to be included in both of these volumes, the selected ZNE projects are required to have a minimum of one year of measured (and verified) energy consumption and energy production data, ideally on a monthly basis and broken down by category of use. Since there is no formal ZNE certification process focused exclusively on this performance criterion[2], the projects in these two volumes were subjected to a careful review of their performance records and, with one exception, confirmed to be operating in a *net positive* mode[3]. (The one exception is Case Study No. 11, The Exploratorium, a unique project in many ways that is very close to ZNE performance after its first full year of operation and that is expected to achieve ZNE in the near future. See the discussion of this special project in this Volume 2.)

With the single exception of The Exploratorium, the selected building projects represent standard building types found in urban and semi-urban areas—office space, educational facility,

---

[1] As in Volume 1, the definition of "zero-net-energy", or ZNE, in Volume 2 is taken to be *Site ZNE*. That is, the amount of energy used by the building over the course of a year is equal to the amount of energy supplied by the on-site renewable energy system. This is the net-metering definition best understood by the public. There are other definitions of ZNE, most notably the nationally-adopted *Source ZNE* and the California building code metric of *Time-Dependent Valuation ZNE*. See the detailed discussion of these metrics in the Introduction to Volume 1.

[2] Nevertheless, it is worth noting that two of the five projects in Volume 2 are certified by the *International Living Future Institute* as *"Net Zero Energy"*, although the requirements for such certification go beyond the energy balance and include other sustainability requirements as well as a prohibition against use of any natural gas (therefore no renewable energy "offsets" allowed in the energy accounting).

[3] *Net Positive* means that the building is producing more renewable energy on-site than it is consuming during that year of data collection.

museum, public library. This volume provides an opportunity to examine the issues associated with building renovations—taking an older building and revamping it entirely to perform at a ZNE level. Four of the five projects in this volume are in fact renovations of existing structures. As such, cost issues were paramount with these projects and it is interesting to compare the cost basis of design decisions in each case.

Focus Issues for the Case Study Buildings of Volume 2

Certain problem issues were identified in the first generation of ZNE buildings, some of which turned out to be common to almost all of the case study buildings discussed in Volume 1. Not surprisingly, these issues were creating barriers to the ready adoption of the ZNE building design approach even for interested and willing owners.

Chief among these early issues was the general inadequacy of the several building control systems to communicate properly in order to optimize the coordinated operation of energy-efficient sub-systems, whether involving windows, shading, HVAC components, lighting or equipment. In the new generation of smart buildings designed to achieve ZNE performance, examples of which are included in Volume 2, a relatively sophisticated sequence of operations is usually employed, one that is highly responsive to varying outdoor conditions such as air temperature, solar intensity and wind conditions, and the indoor occupancy requirements. To accomplish this successfully and reliably, the various control systems need to have common communication protocols and be integrated with an overall master control system.

This understanding of the issue has led to both better control technologies and early engagement with the issue during the design phase of the project. The positive results can be seen in the new generation of ZNE buildings, five of which are documented here in Volume 2.

A second issue that emerged in the first wave of ZNE buildings was the matter of affordability. Once it was demonstrated that ZNE buildings could be realized in the normal built environment with the correct alignment of energy-efficient design and high-productivity renewable energy systems, the next task was to understand the most cost-effective ways of doing this. With the movement in California toward ZNE building code requirements in 2020 (residential) and 2030 (non-residential), and the interest in ZNE building design in general, the affordability of ZNE design features and systems has become a focus of discussion. The case study buildings of this Volume 2 provide a good opportunity to compare both design strategies and financial models for design decision-making.

• Control Systems for Zero Net Energy Buildings

The inadequacy of standard building control systems for the typical level of sophistication of the operation of ZNE buildings has been observed and lamented by many designers. Early ZNE projects were beset by problems of communication between building sub-systems that had different communication protocols built into them. The issue is derived from the lack of a universal communication software for all major building control system applications.

There have been attempts to create such a universal software, but these have devolved into three principal types that are not compatible with each other in integrated building applications: *BACnet* (a protocol developed by ASHRAE and published in 1995), *Modbus* (published by Schneider Electric in 1979 and now managed by Modbus Organization) and *LonWorks* (created by Echelon Corporation and accepted by ANSI in 1999). Manufacturers generally design equipment around one of these communication protocols and sometimes modify the software to improve the operation of their individual product, making integration of systems even more difficult.

In a building that attempts to integrate automatic window operation for free cooling, shade operation, weather measurement, daylight sensors, light controls and aspects of HVAC operation, the reliability of the various control systems to perform as intended is not really possible. This is obviously particularly acute for buildings that are designed around passive systems for ZNE performance.

In 2015, a detailed study and evaluation of state-of-the-art building control systems was carried out by the New Buildings Institute on behalf of CABA (Continental Automated Buildings Association), driven by the concern about the state of affairs with building control systems. The results of the study were published in 2015[4], confirming this problem for ZNE buildings and the need for a change in this part of the building industry.

(Below, this page) Custom-designed master control system for the Packard Foundation Headquarters Building. (See Case Study No. 1 in Volume 1, *Zero Net Energy Case Study Buildings*.)

In practical terms, this major issue can be overcome by introducing a "master control system", sometimes called an "omni-controller", a software package that is a form of communications translator that controls and manages the individual control systems. This was recognized in

[4] Higgins, C., Miller, A., Lyles, M., "Zero Net Energy Controls: Characteristics, Energy Impacts and Lessons Learned Research Report", November 2015, *http://www.caba.org/CABA/Research/Zero-Net-Energy-Buildings.aspx*.

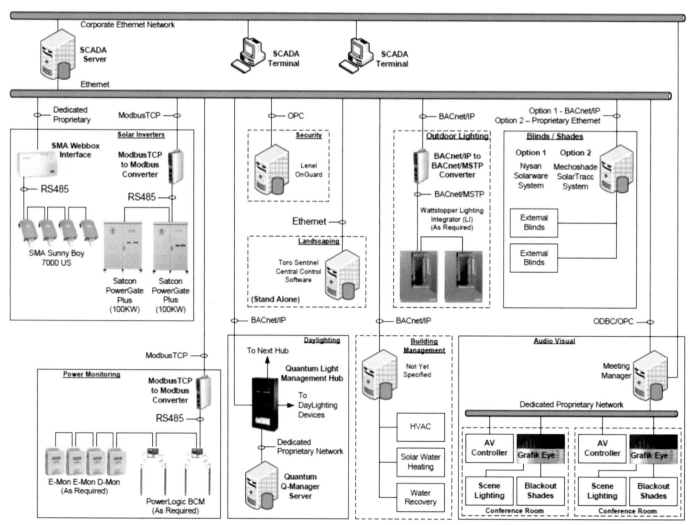

a ZNE building designed in 2008-2010, the Packard Headquarters Building (documented in Volume 1), and the client utilized its own IT staff to modify some existing industrial control software and to develop such a master control system for the project. (See illustration on facing page.) This is a custom system designed specifically for this project, but it was one of the first applications of the concept and has proved to be very successful in the operation of this building.

Since then, master control systems for the integration of building controls have been developed commercially, although modification and adaptation are still required for each specific project. As more building sub-systems become "smart" and are addressable by such systems, as expected with the advent of the *Internet of Things (IOT)*, such a master control system will become standard in building applications. Some of these systems are proprietary, but there are now open, non-proprietary systems currently available as well. These systems mark a significant improvement in the state-of-the-art and a valuable tool for the design and operation of highly energy-efficient buildings. (See illustration below.)

The arrival of this type of system is an important technical advance and it also heralds the importance of a new role on the design team—the "master system integrator", or simply the "integrator". This is the design engineer or technician who programs the basic software of the master controls system for the seamless integration of all the component control systems used to operate the building at maximum efficiency. It is important that this specialist participate in the design development of the ZNE building and continue in that role through early occupancy, working with the commissioning agent to ensure reliable operation of all energy-related sub-systems per the design intent.

Three of the case study buildings documented in Volume 2 incorporated master control systems that were programmed by a system integrator, who was added to the project team for just this purpose. One project used a proprietary master system, while the two others used a non-

(Below, this page) Non-proprietary master control system used for the IBEW-NECA Training Facility. (See Case Study No. 8 in Volume 2, *Zero Net Energy Case Study Buildings*.)

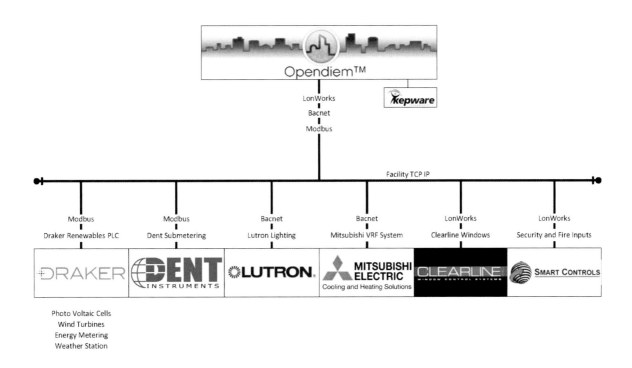

proprietary system; all three experienced good operational results. (See Case Study Nos. 7, 8 and 9.) The remaining two case study buildings, without the inclusion of a master control system, experienced operational difficulties in one case (Case Study No. 10) and data access and collection issues in both cases (Case Study Nos. 10 and 11).

A side benefit of integrating the control system communications is that the system can also be programmed to provide ready access to recorded data, including information beyond simple energy use data. With the proper energy metering setup, energy performance monitoring is simply done and typically accessible via an online dashboard. There are obvious advantages in having this information with regard to improved energy efficiency of operations during occupancy and communication of performance successes to the building occupants.

The case study buildings documented in Volume 2 have benefited from the advance in control system technologies and point the way for future projects with respect to essential ZNE building sub-systems and design strategies.

• *Financial Models for Decision-Making in the Design of Zero Net Energy Buildings*

With few exceptions, every project has cost constraints that drive decision-making in the design of new buildings or renovations. A ZNE building is generally assumed to have a higher initial cost—after all, an entire renewable energy system is usually installed—which is offset over time with the large savings in energy cost. The questions often asked are about how much higher the construction budget must be compared to a "standard" building and how much time before this extra investment is paid back.

Both the questions and the answers are actually more nuanced than this. On the *question* side, for example, the construction budget is derived from many aspects of the building's makeup and a prioritization of expenditure could affect the allocation toward ZNE as a base item. Or some features may have energy-efficiency implications as well as other types of design benefits for the occupants, such as daylighting elements—how would this cost be allocated in a financial analysis for determining ZNE "feasibility" if there are parallel benefits. As another example of the complexity of the question, it has also been shown that a strong passive design approach to a building results in such smaller climate control equipment, that the result is actually a much *less* expensive HVAC plant for a ZNE building employing those strategies.

On the *answer* side, the "right" financial analysis process may not be clear. Aside from the discussion among financial analysts about the appropriate metric to use for *life cycle cost analysis* or *LCCA* (payback period, return on investment or ROI, and others) as well as interest rate and energy cost inflation rate, the client needs to consider the types of "investment" in a ZNE building project appropriate to its situation. For a client that is not holding the building for any length of time, these metrics will be different than for a client that has a specified time period (say a lease period) or for a client that will own the building for long, undetermined period of time. The criteria for design decisions will be quite different in each case.

The case studies documented in Volume 2 each elaborate on this issue of cost constraints and the financial criteria used for design decisions. The differences in each case are clear and demonstrate the complexity of the issue. Case Study No. 10, the West Berkeley Branch Library, is an example of a public project with a fixed budget, which required all ZNE design features to be treated like every other aspect of the project. In such public projects, there is typically no mechanism of providing additional funds that can be "paid back" from future cost savings due to the ZNE features.

In Case Study No. 7, the DPR Construction Office Building, the client chose its 10-year lease as the restriction controlling the payback period for any ZNE design feature installed as part of the tenant improvements in this renovation project. The most interesting example, however, is Case Study No. 9, the Speculative Office Building at 435 Indio Way, which was subject to a meticulous financial investment model that proved that the ZNE building design would actually be *more profitable* as an investment than a standard building design. The financial argument is sufficiently compelling that it is included as a separate sidebar discussion of the topic.

Ultimately, when ZNE building design is the standard and required for all new buildings, the financial analysis of alternative design features and strategies will also become standard and similar to the process used today by project designers to meet project budgets and provide the best product for their clients.

Case Study Projects ▷

CASE STUDY NO. 7

DPR Construction Office Building

PHOTO: DREW KELLY

DPR Construction Office Building
Case Study No. 7

Data Summary

Building Type: Office

Location: San Francisco, CA

Gross Floor Area: 24,010 gsf
(including tenant space of 4,000 gsf)

Occupied: May 2014

Energy Modeling Software:
OpenStudio 1.4

Modeled EUI (Site):
25.8 kBtu/sf-year

Measured EUI (Site):
22.4 kBtu/sf-year (May 2014 —
June 2015)

**On-Site Renewable Energy
System Installed:**
118 kW (DC) Solar PV

**Measured On-Site Energy
Production (Electric):**
157,000 kWh/year
26.8 kBtu/sf-year (May 2014 —
June 2015)

**Measured Solar Thermal
Production:**
3,400 kWh/year
0.6 kBtu/sf-year (May 2014 —
June 2015)

Owner/Client
DPR Construction

Design Team

Architect: FME Architecture +
Design, San Francisco, CA

Structural Engineer: Paradigm,
San Francisco, CA

*Mechanical/Electrical/Plumbing
Systems Design and Energy
Analyst:* Integral Group, Oak-
land, CA

Lighting Design:
DPR Construction

Commissioning Agent:
Integral Group, Oakland, CA

Master System Integrator:
Honeywell

General Contractor
DPR Construction

The *DPR Construction Office Building* in San Francisco is one of three similar zero-net-energy (ZNE) renovation projects included in this monograph (Case Study Nos. 7, 8 and 9). These three exemplary projects provide an opportunity to compare design strategies as they are influenced by their respective urban settings, client goals and, particularly for these three case studies, their financial objectives.

Since these three buildings are basically set in the same coastal marine climate zone and are roughly the same size and type of building, the effects of these other factors become apparent in the final designs. The similarities of the design approaches and the challenges encountered are informative on a comparative basis.

Background

DPR Construction is a national commercial general contractor and construction manager with ZNE office buildings in San Francisco, Phoenix and San Diego. Notably, the firm was the general contractor for the Packard Foundation Headquarters, one of the first ZNE buildings to be completed and certified as performing at ZNE. (See Case Study No. 1 in Volume 1 of *Zero Net Energy Case Study Buildings*.) This project demonstrated first-hand to the company the feasibility of building ZNE facilities using standard building technologies and procedures.

Partly as a result of this experience, the company adopted a corporate mission to advocate for ZNE projects. The firm's leaders determined to start with their own office facilities as both a proving ground and a demonstration of the company's ability to deliver such projects to its clients. This commitment had two specific practical consequences: (1) confirmation that a ZNE facility is equally feasible for an existing building renovation as for new construction; (2) establishment of practical financial constraints that can be met in this context of targeting ZNE, comparing favorably to a non-ZNE approach to a building renovation.

The company undertook this first with its San Diego office then with its Phoenix office building, where it garnered more experience with integrated ZNE design and construction while successfully delivering office spaces that perform today at ZNE level. Its third in-house project in this vein was its San Francisco office, the subject of this Case Study No. 7.

DPR Construction had been in a two-story leased space of about 12,000 sq. ft., located near the San Francisco waterfront close to downtown. The company looked to relocate to a larger space, with the requirement that the building could accommodate enough solar photovoltaic panels (PV) to support the ZNE goal. The ZNE goal was primary, even if it meant leaving the neighborhood after 17 years. Fortunately, a former industrial warehouse building became available in the area and quick design studies confirmed adequate roof geometry for the likely size of the PV system.

The building had some historic significance that DPR wanted to respect, but it was not formally registered as such, eliminating any historic code requirement or review process. The building contained 24,000 sq. ft. on two levels, which allowed for expansion of DPR space and the possibility of small tenants in the interim.

DPR Construction Office Building: General Vicinity Plan

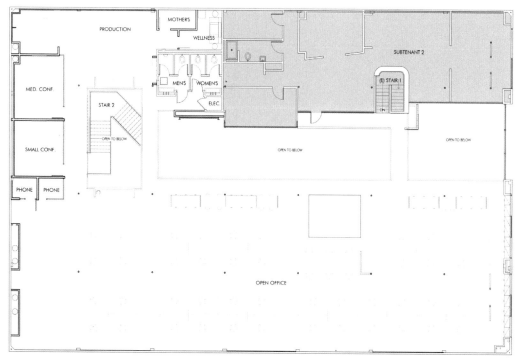

SECOND FLOOR

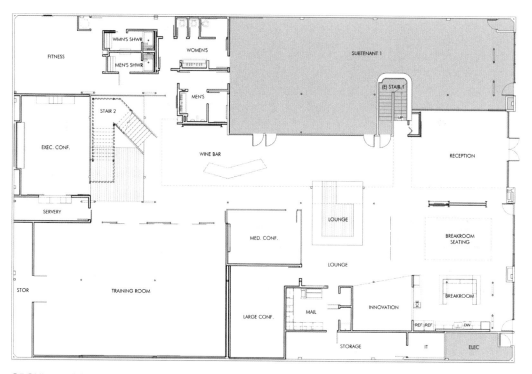

GROUND FLOOR

DPR Construction Office Building: Floor Plans

The building owner was approached for sale of the property, but the response was negative. DPR then negotiated a 10-year lease with terms that would allow substantial building improvements supporting the ZNE performance goal. The owner agreed to a below-market rental rate in exchange for the amount of tenant improvements that DPR proposed for the ZNE renovation. The offset of the rental cost permitted a reasonable scope of building improvements toward the ZNE goal. Also, with DPR's internal requirement that any higher cost item pay back the extra investment within the 10-year lease period, the financial parameters of the renovation were set.

As a side note, the "investment" by the owner of the building, namely the lower rental rate in exchange for the tenant improvements carried out by DPR, has resulted in a significant increase in the value of the property.

Design Process and Low Energy Design Strategies

Every design alternative was evaluated for energy reduction versus cost, with the decisions finally based on the fit with the financial parameters established in advance. Specific examples in this regard are mentioned in the detailed description of the different ZNE design strategies, which follows below.

DPR was able to capitalize on its expertise as a construction manager, as well as the capability to be its own general contractor for this renovation project. They used a design-build process and a team of designers who were familiar with the company and its ZNE design goal. As a result, the design and documentation process was automatically an integrated approach.

In addition, using its construction management team, the company was able to employ successfully an aggressively accelerated schedule. The design of the renovation began in October

Interior View of Atrium

PHOTO: DREW KELLY

2013 and construction was completed in May 2014, a period of roughly 8 months. This amazing schedule included all permitting processes as well.

The low-energy design strategies selected therefore are based on essential contribution to the ZNE performance goal using proven building technologies, consistency with the financial parameters for the project and the practical ability to be incorporated into the building within the highly accelerated schedule. As the results shown below confirm, the project successfully achieved ZNE performance within these highly limiting constraints.

Planning Concept and General Design Considerations

Other project goals that influenced the general planning concept for this renovation were firm-cultural. The company's previous space, which had a sharp division of two separate floors, led to a hierarchic sensibility that was not consistent with that desired by the firm's staff and leaders. The renovated space therefore was planned with openness and a strong spatial connection between the two floors. This social and cultural design objective of connection and transparency also supports the idea of daylight penetration and dispersion to all spaces, as well as the possibility of natural ventilation and/or "night flush" (precooling the space with night air).

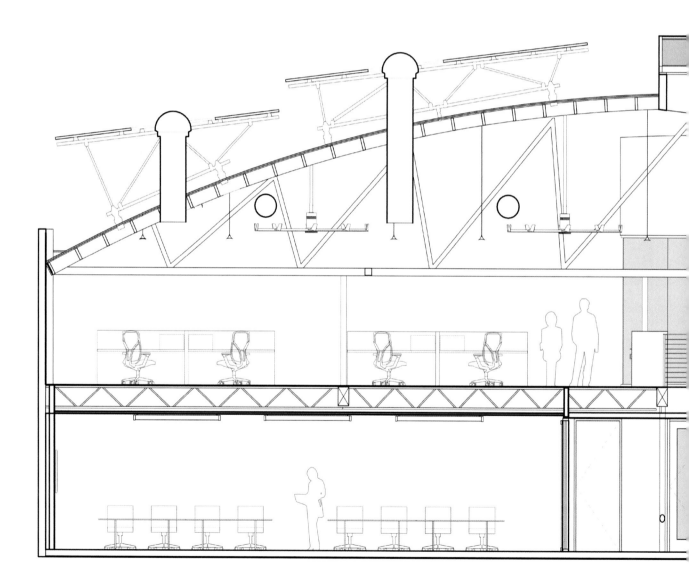

DPR Construction Office Building: North-South Section

The general design response to this concept with the existing building was to remove many of the existing interior elements that enclosed the two levels or blocked views and large skylights, and to maintain the large floor opening below two large existing industrial roof skylights. This can be seen in comparison of "before" and "after" views of the same interior spaces.

To maximize use of the daylight available in the center of the building, spaces needing controlled lighting or having only intermittent use, such as conference rooms, small meeting spaces and the staff exercise room, are located away from this central area or under the connecting stairs. Occupied staff areas are located primarily on the second level, with close access to the daylighting via roof apertures, both existing and new.

BEFORE

The net effect of the strong effort to improve visual connection between levels and open up the middle of the building from first floor to roof skylights is to maximize daylight penetration from the roof to the most intensely occupied spaces but also to support the branding of the company for openness and communication.

It is notable that the building includes a tenant space, which is entirely included within the ZNE boundary of the building. The tenant is aware of the ZNE goals for the building and their participation in meeting those goals.

AFTER

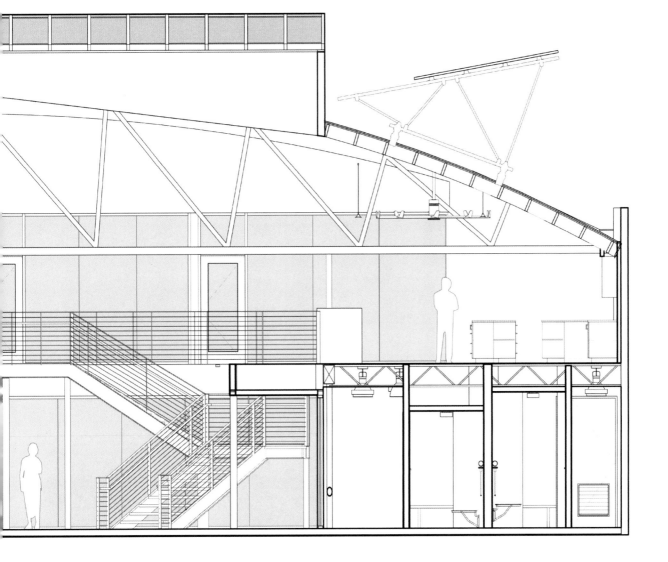

Rough Sizing the On-Site Renewable Energy Supply

The basic concept of a ZNE building is defined as an annual balance of the energy use of the building with the on-site renewable energy supply. In urban locations with strong site limitations, this means that the limitations on the energy supply have to be determined first, so that target annual energy consumption due to the standard loads can be established for the design. This was the case with this case study project, where both solar shading by nearby buildings and the self-imposed design constraint of respecting the general image of the historic old building set a limit on the size of the PV panel arrays.

The study of the sizing of the solar arrays and integration with daylight apertures is described in detail in the discussion below of the design of the on-site renewable energy supply system. This sizing study resulted in a preliminary determination of the total on-site energy supply over the course of a year given the likely size of the solar photovoltaic panel array and the output of the specified panel. This in term set the preliminary design target EUI[1] for the building at 24. This would be the upper limit on the allowable annual energy consumption of the building by all sources of energy use.

It is noted here because of its influence on the various decisions in the early design phase about building envelope, lighting and plug load management.

---

[1] EUI = *Energy Use Intensity*, equal to the energy used over the course of a year in units of thousands of Btu's per unit area of occupied floor space in the building: *kBtu/sq.ft. per year.*

PHOTO: TED VAN DER LINDEN

Building Envelope

There are substantial constraints on the ZNE design strategies associated with the building envelope. As in many urban locations, the neighboring buildings are taller than the project building, in this case casting shadows from the south and west. This reduces the effective roof area available for solar PV panels. Furthermore, given the area's zoning limitations, the neighboring buildings are also built on the lot lines with no setback, and no openings are allowed in any walls except for the street façade. Therefore, the only daylight openings possible are roof apertures and the street-facing windows. The implication, as well, is that natural ventilation would likely be possible only with a special feature such as a thermal chimney, an expensive item if it serves only that function and also a highly visible one.

The urban context, therefore, was simultaneously limiting the effect of low-energy strategies like daylighting and natural ventilation while also capping the possible availability of on-site renewable energy through solar PV systems. This is actually a common situation with ZNE design in urban settings.

Added to these design issues was the desire to respect the original structural elements and related interior features due to the historic nature of the building itself. This design decision primarily affected the roof since it was determined that the roof structure would have to be reinforced to support the solar PV panel arrays. In addition, the roof insulation level needed to be increased significantly to reduce the energy consumption for heating and cooling, given that the roof is by far the largest surface of the building envelope.

(Below) Solar analysis of shading effect of neighboring buildings, using DesignBuilder 3.0. (Courtesy of Integral Group)

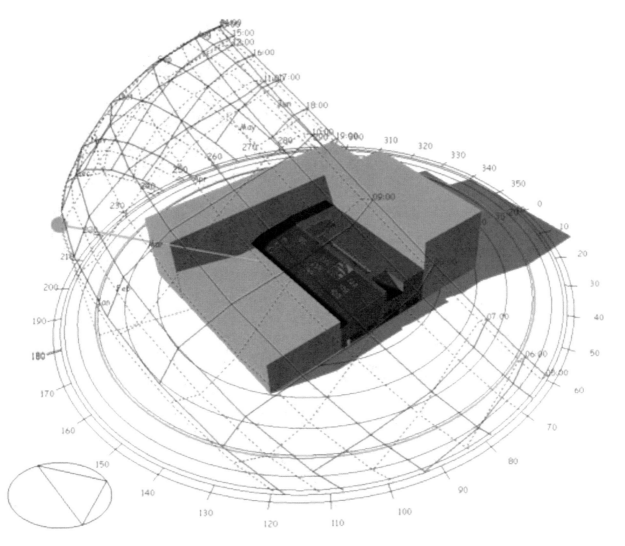

Diagram courtesy of Integral Group

For design reasons, namely to avoid the "pillowing" appearance of insulation added to the underside of the roof sheathing, the insulation was applied to the exterior in the form of a spray foam roofing system. The overall thickness is 4", providing an R-value of 24. The foam also has a UV reflective coating with a solar reflectance of 83% to provide a "cool roof" effect where exposed to the sun.

In addition, structural reinforcement was done with new steel components that resemble the original steel trusswork. These two design approaches for the roof systems preserved the original appearance of the roof structure from the interior while providing the optimum thermal characteristics for that large part of the building envelope.

The concrete building walls, on the other hand, were left untouched and uninsulated. This decision was based on the cost of retrofitting with insulation, which would have to be done from the interior since there is no access to the exterior lot-line walls, versus

the energy use reduction that would result. The energy savings as calculated from early phase energy modeling did not meet the financial parameters established at the start of design. In addition, with this kind of retrofit some rentable floor area would be lost and the building appearance would be altered to some degree.

The exterior wall facing the street, containing a large area of single-pane industrial sash, was also left in its original state for the same reasons. The cost of replacing the original glass with a new double-glazed storefront that resembled the original was deemed to be beyond the limits established for the financial performance of the renovation.

The insulation values established for the renovation and energy modeling exercise were R = 24 for the roof and R = 3 for the walls, with the single-glazing thermal value for the east-facing window area.

PHOTO: DREW KELLY

PHOTO: DREW KELLY

Daylighting and Electric Lighting

Given that the building is one or two stories with a large single roof area above occupied space, as well as the general abundance of natural light in a mild marine climate, daylighting coupled with LED electric light fixtures is the key low-energy design strategy for this project. Challenges were posed again, however, by neighboring site constraints, the blanketing of the roof with the solar panel arrays, and the desire for a light touch to the existing roof for historic reasons.

The roof included two very large industrial skylights over the central two-story open space and, while a source of (over-) abundant daylight locally, they were also a source of great glare. This would have caused an excessive use of interior electric lighting to overcome this problem, so some design modification of the skylights or their interior surround was needed.

These large skylights were to be preserved in appearance for historic reasons, so the company opted to replace the glazing with double-glazed panels rather than install solid diffusing panels or canopies. Great value was also placed on the ability for occupants to see the sky, with cloud movement and the change in light during the day. So, a solution was devised to replace the single-pane skylight glazing with insulated dynamic glass[2] panels in the rectangular sections, which would still allow view out to the sky above while providing glare control and lower solar heat gain. After some post-occupancy tuning, the most comfortable and effective energy-saving levels of the adjustable tinting were set for the spaces below the two skylights.

---

[2] *Dynamic glass* or electrochromic glass is electronically tintable, so that the solar heat gain and light transmission of the glass can be set at a pre-programmed level or through instant control via a portable device. A light sensor reading outside the glass panel is compared to the desired interior condition; the glass system then sets the tint based on the preferred interior light condition for minimal glare and best daylight levels. The glass is therefore tuned to the space.

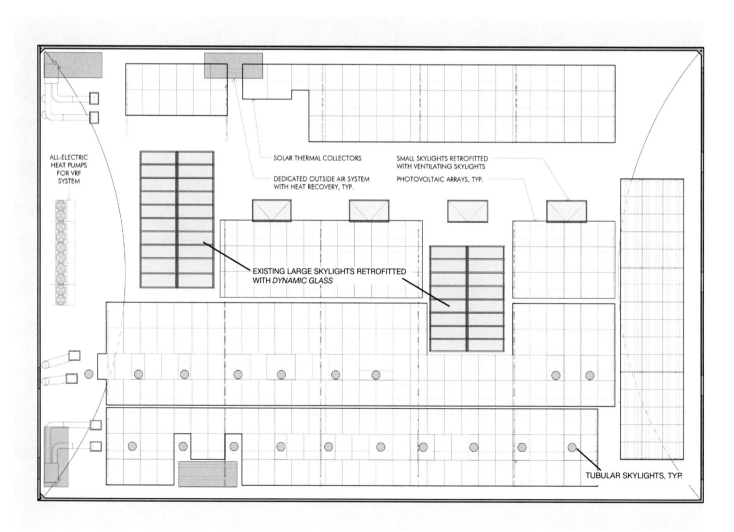

ALL-ELECTRIC HEAT PUMPS FOR VRF SYSTEM

SOLAR THERMAL COLLECTORS

DEDICATED OUTSIDE AIR SYSTEM WITH HEAT RECOVERY, TYP.

SMALL SKYLIGHTS RETROFITTED WITH VENTILATING SKYLIGHTS

PHOTOVOLTAIC ARRAYS, TYP.

EXISTING LARGE SKYLIGHTS RETROFITTED WITH *DYNAMIC GLASS*

TUBULAR SKYLIGHTS, TYP.

It is noteworthy that the east side of the skylight glazing is operated differently from the west side, which allows tuning to the brightness of the sky in different directions.

The cost of this glass technology was relatively high, but because so many design objectives were achieved with it, the company opted to make the investment in this case.

In addition to these two significant shaped skylights, there were eleven old standard flat rectangular skylights that had excessive heat loss via single glazing. Seven of these were removed in the area planned for the solar panels and four existing skylights along the north side of the roof were simply replaced with new openable residential-type skylights, equipped with insulated glazing.

These four smaller skylights are by design only manually openable, making them unsuitable for night flush operation to pre-cool the building during the cooling season. This is an example of another design decision made based on the financial parameters of the project: not enough energy was saved according to the energy modeling via night flush operation to justify the added cost of having the skylight opening controlled by the BMS[3].

Not so incidentally, the San Francisco Fire Department requires a four-foot clear walking area around skylights, which greatly impacts the overall size of the possible solar panel array. This requirement eliminated the possibility of distributing new standard skylights over the entire roof to provide daylight to the occupied space below. Thus, the four replacement skylights on the north side of the roof are the only ones used in this project for daylighting. Fortunately, however, the SF Fire Department does not have the same requirement for *tubular skylights*[4], which can provide substantial daylight when the use of skylights is limited, making this daylighting device a good solution for tight urban sites with limited access to sun and sky.

Given their relatively small diameter, the tubular skylights could be located in the middle of a solar panel array without significantly reducing the available area of that array. For this urban renovation project, therefore, a distributed set of tubular skylights became an integral part of the daylighting solution. The number and layout of the tubular skylights were determined by a daylighting analysis[5], which indicated the right distribution to achieve a minimum of 20 footcandles at the work surface most of the time.

The tubular skylights in this project are not adjustable via dimming. To add a dimming feature would have added cost and internal visibility to the tubular skylight hardware, both of which were rejected by DPR for the financial and historic reasons. Light levels in the tubular skylight area of the second floor have been measured at a glare-free 80 footcandles in summer and 20 footcandles in winter. In the latter case, the task level lighting is raised by electric LED fixtures operating at a very low level. This overall lighting design solution is rated as very comfortable by the building occupants.

PHOTO: TED VAN DER LINDEN

---

[3] BMS: *Building Management System*—the computer-based control system for the mechanical and electrical equipment in the building.

[4] *Tubular skylights* are tubular daylighting devices that use internally reflective metal tubes to transmit daylight to interior spaces from the transparent end of the tube at roof level.

[5] Daylighting analysis was done using AGI32 software

Solar photovoltaic arrays with tubular skylights at roof (Photo, *below left*; section drawing *below right*.)

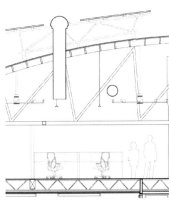

Natural Ventilation

As noted, without openings on three sides of the building cross ventilation is not possible and draft-induced ventilation via the roof was deemed too costly for the amount of energy saved. As a result of this analysis during the design and modeling phase, natural ventilation and night flush operation were eliminated as possible low-energy design strategies.

During the first year of building operation, however, energy-use monitoring indicated that the cooling energy demand was higher than that indicated in the modeling. It appears that a night flush operation may have been useful in general as a low-energy cooling strategy. However, the HVAC system is not a standard VAV system (see discussion below), which has the ability to move 100% outside air through the building, so a further retrofit to accommodate night flush is not really practical at this point.

Heating, Ventilating and Cooling Systems

The design approach to the HVAC system follows the general set of strategies common to many low-energy building designs:

- Utilize highest efficiency heating and cooling equipment;
- Minimize electricity-driven fan use;
- Reduce energy use due to sheer amount of air ductwork to and from a building central plant (i.e., employ distributed *dedicated outside air system* (DOAS) units in lieu of a central plant);
- Utilize low-pressure drop design for the air ducts;
- Decouple air system cooling and fresh air ventilation.

The first strategy is used with the incorporation a single air-source heat pump into a variable refrigerant flow (VRF) system. The latter includes fan-coil units for each zone, providing fast-acting cooling and heating. The system also enables heat to be transferred from spaces requiring cooling to spaces that require heating, allowing for better zoned thermal control of the building overall and higher efficiencies due to this internal heat recovery aspect. This type of system also has excellent partial/low load efficiencies.

The fresh air requirement is met using four *dedicated outside air system* (DOAS) units. These units use 100%-outside-air and demand-controlled ventilation based on CO_2 sensors. This is inherently more efficient than a centralized system because of the tuning of the fresh air requirement to specific demands of separate areas of the building. In addition, the DOAS units avoid the built-in inefficiencies of the large fan power of a central system and long duct runs through ceiling space.

The DOAS units have the possibility of an even higher level of efficiency in this building application. They are equipped with an air-to-air plate heat exchanger, transferring heat from exhaust air to supply air, requiring no additional conditioning at the units because of the mild climate of the San Francisco area.

For cost reasons, only one of the four DOAS units is equipped with a variable-speed fan drive (VFD). The other three are constant volume type. During the design phase, energy modeling indicated only very small energy savings would result if all four DOAS units were VFD type, including daily operation and a potential night flush operation, and the additional cost would not be made up over the period of the 10-year lease. Subsequent building performance measurements now indicate that the building is indeed operating at ZNE or better, so this decision appears to have been justified.

PHOTO: DREW KELLY

The building also capitalizes on another now-standard design consideration for ZNE buildings: the use of large, slow-moving ceiling fans to create a tangible sense of air movement at all times in the space. Studies confirm that occupants feel comfortable at a wider temperature setpoint range if there is perceptible air movement in the space. The large ceiling fans have been employed in the DPR Office space and the experience seems to confirm the study findings.

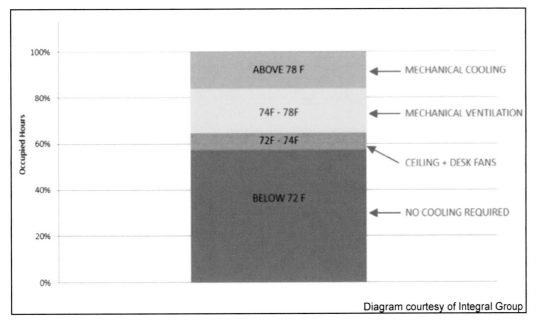

Diagram courtesy of Integral Group

System operation for cooling — Use of large ceiling fans expands the comfort zone due to gentle air movement.

Domestic Hot Water

A solar thermal system for domestic hot water (DHW) was specified and installed. The system consists of two 4'X8' panels and a 120-gallon storage tank with electric backup. There is, therefore, no natural gas fuel used in this building. The non-renewable energy displaced by the solar thermal system is calculated to be 3,400 kWh/year or roughly 0.6 EUI, with a payback (ROI) at 5 years.

Plug Loads

A *plug load* study was performed to identify equipment and large energy consuming systems in addition to standard building operation systems. This study satisfied the obvious need to understand this electric load in order to properly size the on-site solar PV system. New DPR equipment purchasing decisions were also informed by this study.

Control of the plug loads is an essential component of low-energy and ZNE building performance. The DPR Office includes a number of these measures including occupancy sensors at the overhead light fixtures, "smart" plug strips using *plug load management software*[6], measuring all plug load circuits and reporting to a centrally-visible energy dashboard and, finally, a building plug load "kill-switch".

The *kill-switch*, a large red button located adjacent to the main entrance door, is by mutual agreement operated by the last person leaving the building. This essentially eliminates all "parasitic" loads, including various equipment "always-on" operation. The overall control system for the building manages the shutdown to ensure the integrity and easy startup of all systems on the following day. The computer network is operated on a separate system so that normal system updates can be installed overnight. Each workstation has a color-coded outlet indicating the computer system circuit, though most staff take their laptop computers home at night.

Building Control Systems

At the time of the design and construction of this project (2013-2014), an awareness had developed of the potential problem issue of the coordinated design of the different control systems for the various energy systems in zero net energy buildings. (See Volume 1, *Zero Net Energy Case Study Buildings*, for a discussion of the particular problems with control systems in the earlier buildings of case studies No. 1 through No. 6. See also the discussion of this issue in the Introduction to this Volume 2.) Partly driven by this awareness and understanding that control system problems could cause delays with the greatly accelerated schedule, the client partnered with the building management system vendor, Honeywell, to engage a *master system integrator* early in the design-build process.

There are eleven different control systems integrated into the overall master control system. (See the diagram on the facing page.) Because of the pace of the project, the different sub-system vendors had already been selected. The integrator therefore was required to work with the separate communication protocols that were already established for the project. As noted in the Introduction, there are three principal communication protocols in use in the U.S. at this time, two of which are utilized by sub-systems in this building (BACnet and Modbus). Each one was slightly changed by the sub-system manufacturers to suit their purposes, however, so the integrator was required to work with a technician from each manufacturer in order to coordinate the system communications properly.

---

[6] See, for example, https://www.enmetric.com/platform

With the master system in place, all of the individual control systems and building operations can be adjusted and monitored using a dedicated website that hosts the "command and control suite". In addition, information is sent to the public display "dashboard" and the USGBC's new *LEED Dynamic Plaque*. With this system, the information can also potentially be utilized by a cloud-based facilities management service, which uses data analytics to optimize and trouble-shoot the building operations and performance. Given the close tracking of the building performance that DPR is doing at this time, this service is not currently being used.

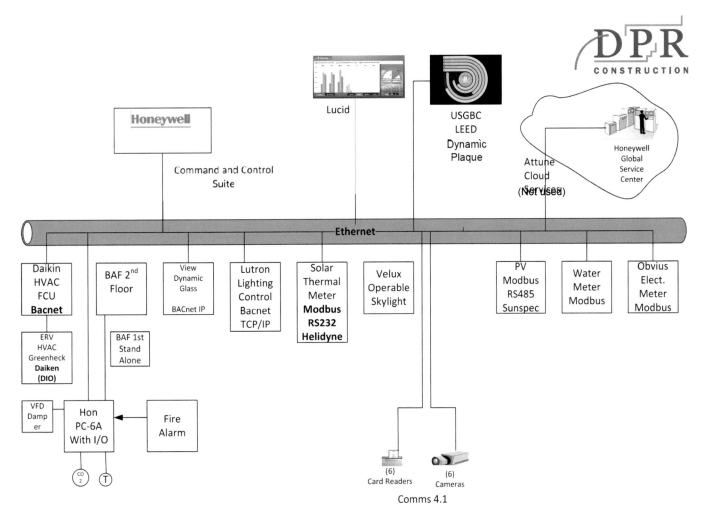

Diagram courtesy of Honeywell

Renewable On-Site Energy Supply

The preliminary sizing of the on-site renewable energy system set a design target for the EUI, which influenced subsequent building design decisions and, according to the energy modeling done of the iterating design solutions, was ultimately achieved. The final design was modeled at an EUI = 25.8 and 118 kW for the full solar photovoltaic system, which has resulted in a better-than-ZNE (i.e., *net positive*) performance for the building. The installed panels are rated at 345 watts (DC) per panel.

The several design iterations included a thorough study of the layout of the PV arrays on the rounded roof, accommodation of the small solar thermal panel array for DHW, inclusion of all daylight-source skylights and solatubes and, finally, avoidance of all shadows from adjacent buildings. This design exercise is typical for all zero-net-energy buildings located in relatively dense urban and suburban areas.

PHOTO: TED VAN DER LINDEN

Two additional contextual factors affected the final design of the roof and the amount of PV panel area that could be installed there. The first was DPR's desire not to allow the PV panel arrays to become a visual distraction from the form and character of the original warehouse building. The second was a desire by DPR not to block sunlight and views from the middle floor of the neighboring five-story building to the north, even though zoning regulations would have allowed this. These factors resulted in a mostly horizontal orientation for most panels, hugging the roof form. One part of the array actually faces east at a slight tilt, where the roof rounds down toward the street façade in that location.

As is the case with standard solar photovoltaic panel installations, only a few percentage points in performance are lost for a horizontal installation as opposed to an optimum performance tilted array. Since panels in horizontal arrays do not cast shadows on adjacent panels in that array, the number of panels that can be fit on to an urban roof is maximized. This delivers more power in general (kW) from the system despite the small loss in efficiency due to panel orientation.

PHOTO: TED VAN DER LINDEN

Energy Design Analysis and Energy Performance:
Modeling versus Post-Occupancy Measurements

Energy Use — Modeling

The energy modeling for the DPR Office Building was carried out using OpenStudio 1.4. The modeling analysis early in the design process showed a total energy use of 151,000 kWh per year, or an EUI of 21.5 kBtu/sq. ft. per year. This was below the original target of EUI = 24.0.

Energy Use — Actual Measurement and Comparison to Modeling Results

Electrical circuits were metered and data results are recorded, accessible via online platform. The energy dashboard in the reception area provides real-time display of energy performance, including the energy produced by the solar PV system. Monitoring began immediately after the building was initially occupied in May, 2014, and a full year of data was collected thereafter.

The measured results show that the building energy use over this year has been less than that indicated by the energy modeling, while the PV panels have produced more than enough electric energy to offset this demand. The actual energy used was 132,000 kWh (EUI = 18.7 kBtu/sq.ft. per year), while the energy produced was 157,000 kWh per year.

Note that the total gross floor area within the "ZNE boundary" includes the tenant space, as does the total amount of energy used and measured. The tenant participates knowledgeably in the energy performance of the building.

The metering system is not set up to distinguish between heating and cooling operation, so the measured data, lumped together in the "Mechanical" category, records both types of energy use. The measurements show for the 2014-2015 period that more energy was used during the cooling season than modeled for that period, while less energy was used during the heating season than indicated by the energy modeling. Since this particular measurement period was a severe drought year, with warmer temperatures and clearer skies than normal, the energy used for heating and cooling would understandably have this pattern compared to the "typical year" weather data used for energy modeling.

A contributing factor to the much lower energy use during the heating season could have been the organized staff efforts to conserve energy, which was undertaken after the first six months of occupancy when the higher energy use for cooling was reported. The latter indicated that ZNE performance might not be achieved in the first year, so DPR staff focused on following suggested practices to reduce unnecessary energy use. (See *Post-Occupancy: Occupant Behavior*, p. 27)

The following pages show the annual energy use (pie-charts) and monthly energy use (bar charts) for both the energy modeling results and the first full year of actual measured performance data for the building. Note that all energy used for heating, cooling, fans, pumps and DHW system is included in the category "Mechanical". The metering is not set up for determining a finer category breakdown for energy consumption since the system heating and cooling come from the same system (the heat pump).

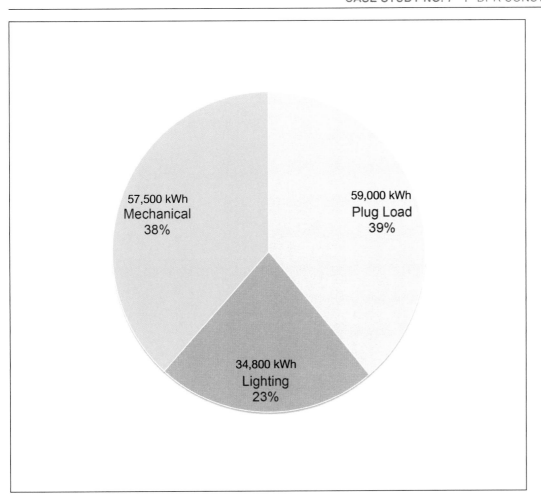

Modeled Energy Use
(Annual)

151,000 kWh per Year
Modeled EUI = 21.5

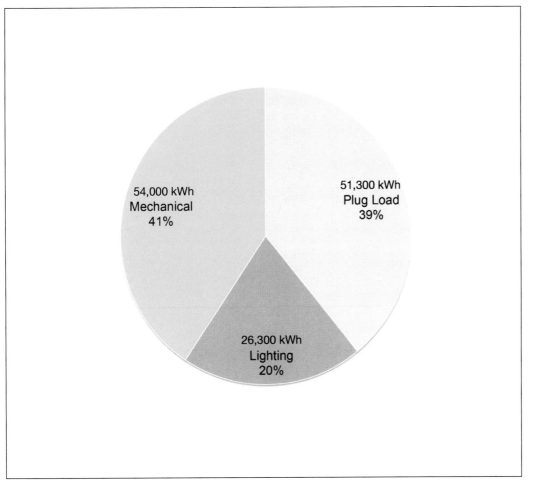

Measured Energy Use
May 2014 - April 2015

132,000 kWh per Year
Actual EUI = 18.7

"Mechanical" =
Heating, Cooling, Ventilation
and DHW

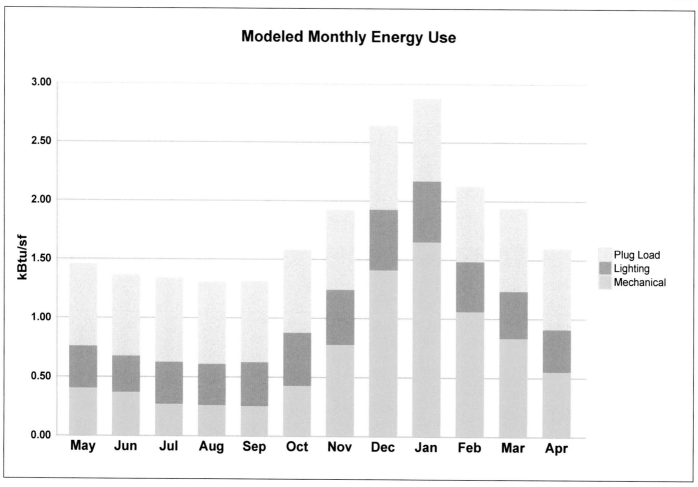

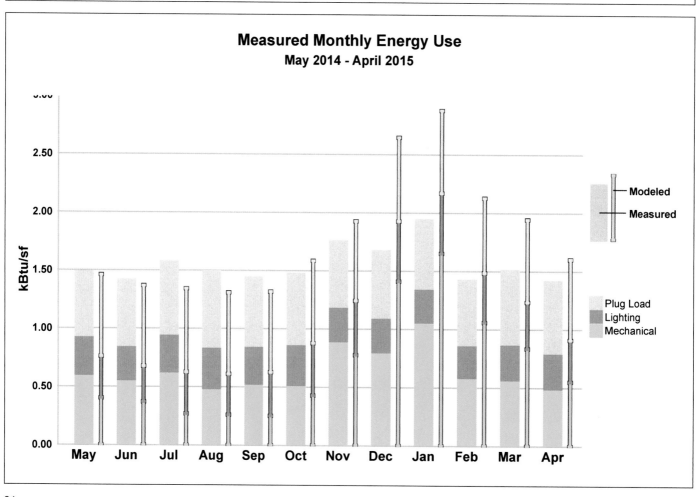

Energy Production versus Energy Use: Zero Net Energy

The measurements recorded during this first year of operation indicate that the building is performing at roughly 20% better than ZNE, which is called "net positive" performance. The chart below shows the energy produced each month by the building's PV system compared with the energy used by the building.

The chart showing *Cumulative Net Energy Performance* over the course of the year (next page) is another graphic indication of *net positive* performance. In this chart, the net production each month (amount of energy produced minus the amount of energy used) becomes the starting point of the following month's net production amount. In this case, since the chart begins in May at the start of summer, the curve goes up at first since the net production is positive in the summer months. The curve then flattens and goes down through the winter months as the solar energy production is poor, turning up again as the sunny spring season begins.

If the building were precisely ZNE for the year, the curve would dip below the zero axis in winter and then just come up and touch the zero axis at the end of the measurement year in April. A precisely-ZNE building would therefore produce a basic S-curve. The chart for the DPR Office Building, however, remains above the zero axis, indicating *net positive* performance.

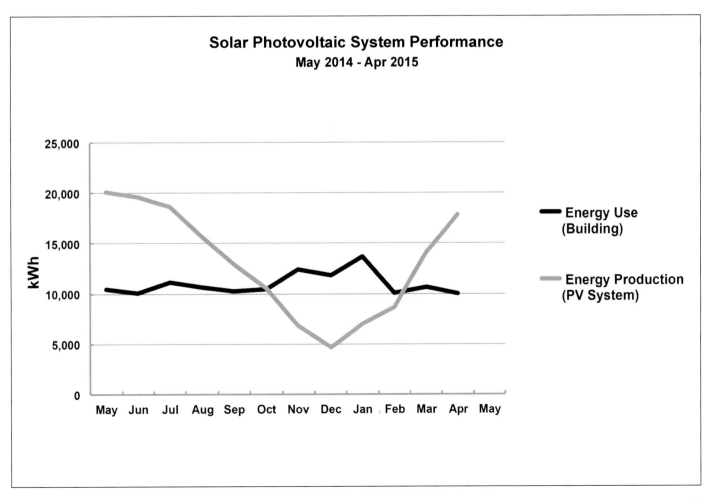

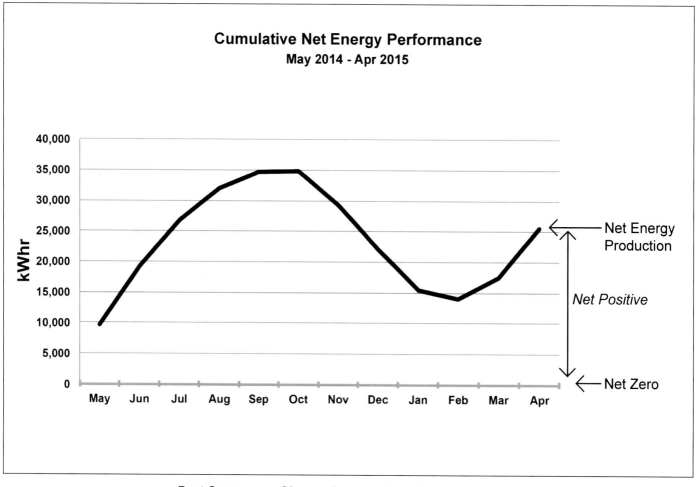

Cumulative Net Energy Performance
May 2014 - Apr 2015

Post Occupancy: Observations and Conclusions

The low-energy design strategies that were incorporated into the design met the financial criteria established for the project. The performance data that started being collected at the occupancy date of May 2014 confirms the achievement of a minimum of ZNE performance for this renovation project in an urban setting, meeting strict financial constraints and an aggressive design and construction schedule.

Post Occupancy: Controls and Monitoring

The issue of accuracy of the meters being used for building energy use continues to be consistent with the case study projects. As noted in early case study discussions in Volume 1, care must be taken to specify the correct size for current transformers (CTs) to ensure correct readings. The conclusion, based on the experience with several case study buildings, is that the meters must be commissioned along with the rest of the building systems. This task is most often not included in the normal base scope of commissioning agents.

In the case of the DPR Construction Office Building, the master system integrator had to work closely with the technicians from the different control systems manufacturers to make sure the controls communications were working properly. Although manufacturers generally adopt one of the three major communication protocols and follow the associated standards, they sometimes "tweak" these protocols to suit their product's functionality and product information sheets are not updated accordingly.

The one control system that could not be integrated was the new skylight opening controls. The new skylights specified were manufactured in Europe and the communication protocols were incompatible with the master control system. These skylights had to be left as manual operation only.

Post Occupancy: HVAC and Commissioning

Early results of measurements of energy use in the first couple of months indicated that more energy was being used in the newly renovated building than the model indicated, to the point that the performance target of ZNE for the first year was not going to be reached. With this information, DPR pushed to complete the commissioning of the building systems and discussed the impact on building operation of occupant behavior with all the staff. With attention to these issues, the subsequent measurements showed an improvement in performance.

One of the operation changes made during the first few months of occupancy was to schedule the HVAC system so that no air conditioning is cycled on during the cleaning period in the evening, when no other activities are scheduled. This eliminated a bump in energy use that was not required for the cleaning staff.

Post Occupancy: Lighting

Daylighting the open office area with the tubular skylights combined with low-level LED light fixtures appears to provide a good level of comfortable, glare-free light, especially for occupants engaged in work on computer screens. (This issue is discussed again in Case Study No. 9, the Speculative Office Building at 435 Indio Way.)

Post Occupancy: On-Site Renewable Energy Systems

While optimizing the design objectives quite well, the flat PV panel arrays require more cleaning than a tilted array. It was also noticed that the east-facing tilted array actually provided a good power boost in the morning, which was useful for the start-up operation.

Obtaining city approvals and avoiding unanticipated delays as the project moved aggressively toward the start of construction became a priority for DPR. City approval for the electrical system was quickly obtained by decoupling the PV system from the electrical permit application. The PV system was submitted later, as an add-on during construction. This also avoided planning approval delays before construction was allowed to begin, which occur occasionally in urban settings due to concerns about the visual impact of PV panel on a roof.

However, when the PV system was added to the project, the utility company, Pacific Gas & Electric Company, notified DPR that the local transformer had to be upsized. The standard lead time for the new transformer was exceedingly long, so a special effort was made to shorten that lead time so that the move-in date could be close to schedule.

Post Occupancy: Occupant Behavior

The case study buildings continue to illustrate the strong influence of occupant behavior on the overall energy use, with low-energy performance improving further with direct involvement and control by motivated occupants. The energy dashboard (photo, *right*) provides regular information about building performance and continues to be an effective communication and motivational tool for staff involvement. DPR also provides each staffperson with a "quick reference" guide about each building feature over which they have individual control. The cards of the guide provides basic information on each feature and various control and use options (*below*).

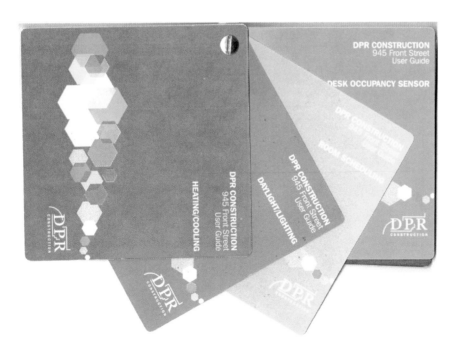

IBEW-NECA JATC Training Facility

PHOTO: CHAD ZIEMENDORF

IBEW-NECA JATC Training Facility
Case Study No. 8

Data Summary

Building Type: Classroom / Office

Location: San Leandro, CA

Gross Floor Area: 45,000 gsf

Occupied: June 2013

Energy Modeling Software: eQuest 3.63

Modeled EUI (Site):
18.0 kBtu/sf-year

Measured EUI (Site):
16.3 kBtu/sf-year (July 2014—June 2015)

On-Site Renewable Energy System Installed:
154 kW (DC) Solar PV-flat panel
12 kW (DC) Solar PV-tracking
12 kW (DC) Wind Turbines

Measured On-Site Energy Production:
267,500 kWh/year
20.3 kBtu/sf-year

Solar Thermal Production: Not measured.

Owner/Client
IBEW Local 595 / National Electrical Contractors Association—Northern California Chapter

Design Team
Architect: FCGA Architects, Dublin, CA

Structural Engineer: Belden Inc., Pleasanton, CA

Mechanical/Electrical/Plumbing Engineer: Belden Inc, Pleasanton, CA

Sustainability Consultant (Energy Modeling): EBS Consultants, San Francisco, CA

Landscape Architect: Gates & Associates, San Ramon, CA

Master System Integrator: Energy Etc, Union City, CA

General Contractor
Novo Construction Company

Like Case Study No. 7, the *IBEW-NECA JATC Training Facility* is an example of a renovation of an existing low-rise building converted from one type of use to another. Whereas the DPR Office project is located in a moderately dense urban setting, Case Study No.8 is in a suburban area of light industrial development, very typical in many communities on the outskirts of metropolitan areas.

These types of renovation projects make interesting case studies since some of the standard ZNE design strategies are limited or simply not possible given the constraints imposed by the nature of the existing building. As these projects demonstrate, many successful design approaches are still possible within the budget limitations. The key to this success lies with good design, involving the continuous referencing of low-energy use as the development and integration of design features proceed.

Background

The project was initiated by the Alameda County Joint Apprenticeship Training Committee (JATC), an organization created to develop the advanced training and education of electrical apprentices. The JATC consists of the International Brotherhood of Electrical Workers Local Union 595 (IBEW) and the Northern California Chapter of the National Electrical Contractors Association (NECA). The organization provides educational and training programs in association with the local community college for electrical apprentices to obtain union certification and for continuing education of already certified electricians as the electrical industry continues to change in response to the technological advances in building design.

In fact, the stated vision for the building is based on the general national goal of training workers for the emerging green building technologies, including renewable energy systems, and preparing them for the changes in the building industry as these technologies develop.

The JATC leadership went further and also proposed that the renovated building be designed to perform at *zero net energy* utilizing the most practical cutting edge technologies, particularly those involving renewable electrical power, communications and control systems. The vision for the building was that it function as a teaching laboratory for electrical workers, not only within the program spaces, but also as demonstrated in the building itself. As part of this vision, the description of the design intent for the A/E team was that the ZNE building features related to electrical systems should be showcased as part of the design and that the building design should illustrate these systems as fundamental to the future of carbon-neutral buildings.

Built in 1981, the existing 45,000 sq. ft. "tilt-up" concrete building was purchased by the IBEW and NECA in 2011 with the plan to renovate it into classrooms, workshops and office space.

(Below) View of the original 1981 building before renovation. (Photo courtesy FCGA Architects)

IBEW-NECA JATC Training Facility: General Vicinity Plan

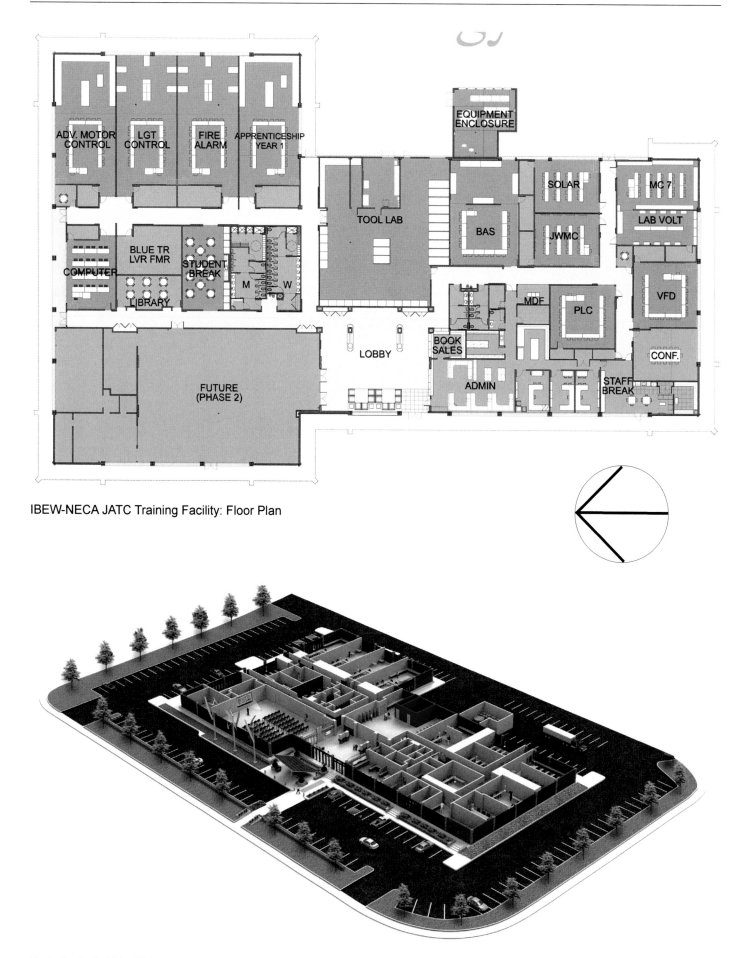

IBEW-NECA JATC Training Facility: Floor Plan

Illustration by Paiching Wei courtesy of the Northern California Sound and Communications NECA-IBEW LMCC

In contrast to Case Study No. 7, the DPR Construction office building, where the client is a tenant with a 10-year lease, the client for this case study is the owner. A market-comparable budget was established for the renovation and design decisions were weighed against cost factors, including life-cycle assessment of low-energy building features and systems.

The JATC leadership hired the design team based primarily on knowledge of the client's programmatic objectives, not with regard to experience with the design of ZNE buildings. As the JATC confirmed its goal of a design integrated with ZNE systems and overall ZNE performance, the sustainability consultant was added to the team to provide ZNE design concepts and analysis. An intensive period of re-design followed to incorporate these concepts and to carry out both technical and financial analyses.

The resulting building was deemed to be so successful in achieving the ZNE-related goals of the project that the client has named the building *The Zero Net Energy Center*.

Design Process and Low Energy Design Strategies

In a process similar to that of Case Study No. 7, life cycle cost assessment was applied to decisions about alternative building features and systems. Also, the existing building itself presented constraints that made normal low-energy features costly to incorporate, ruling them out based on cost criteria. This case study therefore also demonstrates that ZNE performance is still reasonably possible even in the absence of normally prescribed ZNE building characteristics.

A related commonality of the two case studies was the involvement during the design process of the general contractor. In Case Study #7 the client *was* the general contractor, while for this case study, the JATC hired the general contractor primarily to provide pricing for design feature alternatives. Hard bids from the different trades were then submitted to the general contractor when the design phase was completed and bid packages were issued by the design team.

The project therefore followed an *integrated design process* (IDP) among design disciplines as well as close involvement of the general contractor and subcontractors during the entire process. In a further advance of integration of the design and construction processes, the client involved a *master system integrator* beginning in the design phase specifically to coordinate the operational controls for all systems in the building from design through construction and then continuing in a maintenance role through the first years of occupancy. (See the discussion below under "Building Control Systems" for more details about the role of the *master system integrator*.)

Planning Concept and General Design Considerations

The building program developed by the project team includes hands-on classroom spaces (laboratories), workshops, meeting spaces and an office suite for the IBEW-NECA training program. The entire interior of the existing building was gutted and re-planned as the new educational training center. The new spaces are generally organized with the office spaces, classrooms and laboratories at the exterior of the large, one-story floor plate, adjacent to the limited number of windows, with workshops located in the interior.

Because of the large amount of interior space and the relatively large population and equipment use in that space, the cooling load was expected to dominate over heating. As a result, the design team focused on cooling strategies that capitalized on the free cooling available due to the marine climate as well as lighting load reductions through effective daylighting.

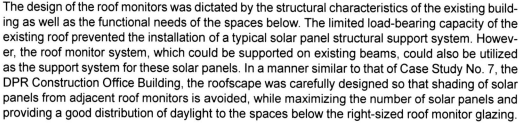

(Above) Clerestory windows installed as part of the renovation.

Building Envelope

The existing building was a typical tilt-up structure with 10-foot deep "mansard"-type overhangs on all sides, single-glazed windows and no insulation on the concrete walls. A band of relatively small clerestory windows was located on all four sides of the perimeter—insufficient for any daylighting given the overhangs but potentially capable of being repurposed for natural ventilation.

The early energy modeling and cost analysis indicated that insulating the walls or replacing the windows with double-glazed units would not improve energy performance enough to justify the cost. This is due in part to the fact that the largest portion of the exterior envelope is the roof; the wall and window area is simply a small fraction of the total.

The roof received a standard code-level of insulation (R-19) applied on the interior surface and a portion of an east-facing wall received an application of an *exterior insulation and finishing system (EIFS)* to repair the old concrete surface. Also, the natural ventilation strategy required the replacement of every second clerestory window with a system-operated double-glazed hopper window, thus upgrading the insulating value of some of the window system. (See "Natural Ventilation" discussion below.) Aside from these measures, the building was left in its original state of a relatively low level of thermal insulation. Other cost effective ZNE design strategies were adopted instead in order to bring the overall energy load down to a level that made ZNE performance realizable.

Daylighting and Electric Lighting

Daylighting was an important design strategy for this renovated building given the large amount of interior floor space, with most program spaces lacking adjacency to the limited number of exterior windows. The principal daylighting design approach is the use of roof monitor arrays, which were also designed to support the solar photovoltaic panels and to provide air outlets for the natural ventilation of these interior spaces. Solatubes are used as a secondary daylighting system, providing daylight principally in the corridor spaces and in those areas where roof monitors are not structurally possible.

The design of the roof monitors was dictated by the structural characteristics of the existing building as well as the functional needs of the spaces below. The limited load-bearing capacity of the existing roof prevented the installation of a typical solar panel structural support system. However, the roof monitor system, which could be supported on existing beams, could also be utilized as the support system for these solar panels. In a manner similar to that of Case Study No. 7, the DPR Construction Office Building, the roofscape was carefully designed so that shading of solar panels from adjacent roof monitors is avoided, while maximizing the number of solar panels and providing a good distribution of daylight to the spaces below the right-sized roof monitor glazing.

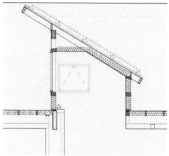

(Above) New roof monitors for daylighting, passive ventilaton and structural support of solar photovoltaic panels.

(Opposite) View of roof monitor array from classroom interior.

In this case study building, the roof monitor glazing is vertical and faces the lower north portion of the sky. There is additional limitation on the view of the sky above due to the structural overhangs on the roof monitors, which are included for waterproofing reasons. The vertical glazing also "sees" the solar PV panels on the roof monitor to the north, which actually provides additional daylight that is reflected back off the panels.

The shape of the roof monitors creates diffuse daylight from these natural and structural exterior daylight sources for the classroom and workshop spaces below. Electrically-operated shades in the monitors are used to reduce the light level when required for A/V presentations.

An initial design idea was to turn one roof monitor in the central café space to face south, connecting it to a large concrete wall for passive solar heating of that one space. The concrete wall proved to be impractical and was eliminated for cost reasons, but the one south-facing roof moni-

tor remains as originally planned, providing some pleasant direct sunlight to the central common space, where diffuse controlled daylight is not really required.

The daylighting is coordinated with the operation of electric lighting, which consists of simple T8 fluorescent lamps in linear pendant light fixtures. The electric lights are dimmed in response to daylight sensor readings and programmed light levels as appropriate for each space. Generally, light levels are set at 50-75 footcandles in workshop spaces and 20 footcandles in computer classrooms. LED light sources are used only in high spaces with industrial area fixtures.

Natural Ventilation

The local marine climate provides for the opportunity for "free cooling" for much of the year, which aligns with the predominant demand for cooling of the many internal spaces. During normal operating hours, sufficient natural ventilation for free cooling is achieved by using the retrofitted openable windows in the clerestory bands at the exterior walls as the air inlets and the operable vents in the sides of the new roof monitors as the air outlets. Air transfer openings are used in internal walls to provide the cooling air to the other interior building spaces using the high operable vents in the roof monitors above those rooms. The height of the roof monitors creates a certain amount of air buoyancy and also a natural drafting effect as exterior breezes pass over the roof.

To make sure that this method of creating airflows through the building is reliable and would work at the level of a room occupant, the design team carried out a CFD analysis ("computational fluid dynamics") for typical spaces. This analysis showed that the desired quantity and path of airflow could be achieved under typical outdoor air conditions at the site.

This natural ventilation approach is designed only for "free cooling" purposes; it is not intended to satisfy minimum fresh air requirements for the building occupants under full heating or cooling operation, so there are no CO_2 sensors in the spaces. When the windows and roof monitor vents are open, the HVAC system is not permitted to operate in heating or cooling mode. The HVAC system fans, however, can move additional untreated cool outside air in specific spaces as needed to augment the naturally drafting ventilation airflow there.

Heating, Ventilating and Cooling Systems

As in Case Study No. 7, the DPR Construction Office Building, the design engineers recognized the importance of avoiding the use of a central HVAC system with large fans and ductwork extending through the building. A distributed approach with smaller fans and smaller local ductwork, the more energy-efficient approach, was adopted. With the JATC Training Facility, however, the nature of the program spaces and the large floor plate of the building can often require heating of one space at the exterior while cooling another space at the interior. This can occur when outdoor air temperatures are moderately low, requiring heat at perimeter spaces, while there are high populations in the interior classrooms that therefore require cooling at the same time. This relative prevalence of simultaneous heating and cooling suggests a split system design for the HVAC system.

An energy-efficient design of a split system, given the preferred distributed approach with local fresh air supply, is to use fluid rather than air to add and remove heat from spaces in the building. This is accomplished using a VRF (variable refrigerant flow) HVAC system, which utilizes a central condensing unit and a smart manifold combined with local fan coil units distributed around the building and serving the different thermal zones. With this system, heat can be removed from zones requiring some cooling and distributed to other zones calling for heating; this can be done with a simple transfer of fluid at low overall use of energy.

The distributed fan coil units have individual outside air inlets to provide fresh air locally, without the need for large and lengthy duct runs. As noted in the discussion of Natural Ventilation, the HVAC system uses a mixed mode operation to make maximum use of free cooling using outside air. When a building zone is in natural ventilation mode, the heating and cooling mode cannot operate. Similarly, when a zone is in heating mode or cooling mode, the minimum required fresh air is introduced at the individual fan coil unit serving that zone. In addition, there is a Night Flush mode of operation, which uses all fan coil units to run at 100% outside air to precool the building at night when outdoor air temperatures are low enough and predicted daytime temperatures will require cooling operation during the following day.

A stand-alone solar thermal system supplies domestic hot water (DHW) for the building.

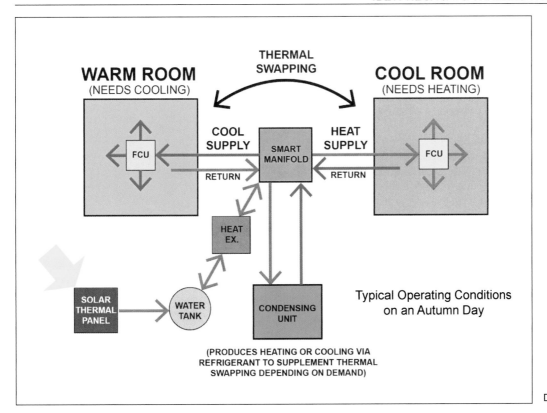

THERMAL SWAPPING

WARM ROOM
(NEEDS COOLING)

COOL ROOM
(NEEDS HEATING)

COOL SUPPLY

HEAT SUPPLY

FCU

SMART MANIFOLD

FCU

RETURN

RETURN

HEAT EX.

SOLAR THERMAL PANEL

WATER TANK

CONDENSING UNIT

Typical Operating Conditions on an Autumn Day

(PRODUCES HEATING OR COOLING VIA REFRIGERANT TO SUPPLEMENT THERMAL SWAPPING DEPENDING ON DEMAND)

Diagram courtesy of FCGA Architects.

PHOTO: CHAD ZIEMENDORF

Plug Loads

Because of the low energy demand achieved through building design, as is typical with ZNE buildings, the plug load for the building is a substantial fraction of the total load. To assist the client in minimizing this energy demand by all the equipment that would be used in the building, the design team analyzed the plug loads in their previous facility and made suggestions about replacing those items that were not at least Energy Star or equivalent.

A major decision with some impact was to replace all desktop computers that would be used as part of the program with laptops and other energy-efficient computer equipment. Given that the building was committed to a ZNE design, a cost study determined that the cost of additional solar PV panels to offset the electrical demand of current program computer equipment would be greater than the cost of simply replacing that equipment.

Other types of electrical equipment used in the training program have a relatively low electric demand or the time of use is short, thus not creating a significant increase in the overall plug load.

(Right) Plug Load survey form used to evaluate equipment energy consumption at the existing facility and estimate plug load total for the new building. (Courtesy of EBS Consultants)

Building Control Systems

At the time of the design and construction of this project (2011-2013), an awareness had developed of the potential problem issue of the coordinated design of the different control systems for the various energy systems in low-energy buildings. (See Volume 1, *Zero Net Energy Case Study Buildings*, for a discussion of the particular problems with control systems in the earlier buildings of case studies #1 through #6. See also the discussion of this issue in the Introduction to this Volume 2.)

Since the client for the JATC Training Center was particularly knowledgeable about electrical systems and the emerging importance of control system design in advanced buildings, a specialty subconsultant, known as the *master system integrator*, was added to the contractor advising team in the design phase to address issues of smart building design and operation, control system commissioning, data collection and performance monitoring. By leading the way in the design process itself for this case study building, the client created a model for an approach to the coordination and design of modern building control systems for advanced low-energy buildings, as well as performance measurement and reporting.

The *master system integrator* coordinated the design of all building subsystem control systems along with the detailed sequence of operations and created a non-proprietary controls network. He also made recommendations about energy metering for all subsystems, including the solar energy production subsystem, and created an overall monitoring program from a commercially available software package[1]. The monitoring program continuously collects all data, some of which is organized into a web-based energy dashboard for display on a flat screen in the building lobby. Other building subsystem data can be accessed at any time for building operation and maintenance purposes using a user-friendly graphical interface.

Once the building construction was completed, the *master system integrator* continued to operate the monitoring program under a facilities maintenance agreement with the client. This continuity from design through early occupancy allowed the master system integrator to suggest operational changes to reduce energy consumption and to trouble-shoot equipment issues during the first two years.

---

[1]*Opendiem*, by Building Clouds.

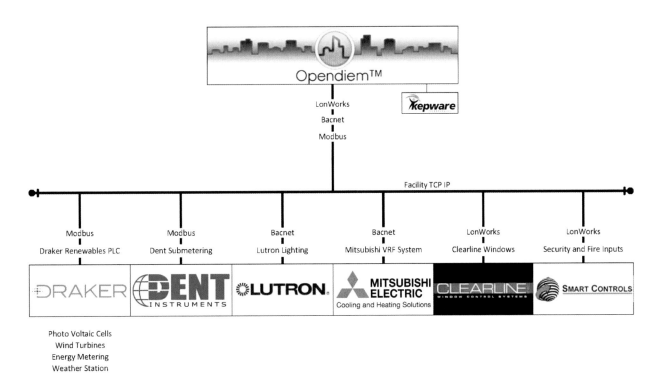

Diagram courtesy of Energy Etc

Renewable On-Site Energy Supply

One of the goals mandated by the client was to showcase advanced building electrical systems, including all forms of on-site renewable energy systems that might be encountered in practice. This would allow electrical apprentices to be trained on all system types. For this reason, three different types of on-site renewable electric energy supply were installed and prominently displayed near the entrance to the building.

1. Solar photovoltaic flat-plate fixed panels, the most common and most cost effective source of on-site renewable electric energy, is the principal system used, generating 154 kW (DC) at peak capacity. These panels cover the roof, mounted on the top of the roof monitors, and are also installed on the "mansard" roof overhangs on the south and west sides of the building.

2. A second system of solar photovoltaic flat-plate panels on a tracking platform, known as the "Tracking Solar Tree®", consists of a billboard-sized platform holding 45 flat PV panels, is tilted at 15° and rotates at the top of its supporting column, following the sun as it moves east to west during the day. Normally used as canopies in parking lots where electric cars will be parked, this structure shades an entry courtyard at the main building entrance.

3. Three wind turbines complete the collection of types of on-site renewable systems and are also installed prominently near the main entrance. Because of the proximity of the Oakland airport, the wind turbines were limited to a sub-optimum height and are generally non-operational, except as needed for instructional purposes.

Real-time energy production data for all three systems can be observed on the energy dashboard display in the entrance lobby.

(Above) Inverter equipment and energy dashboard are prominently displayed.

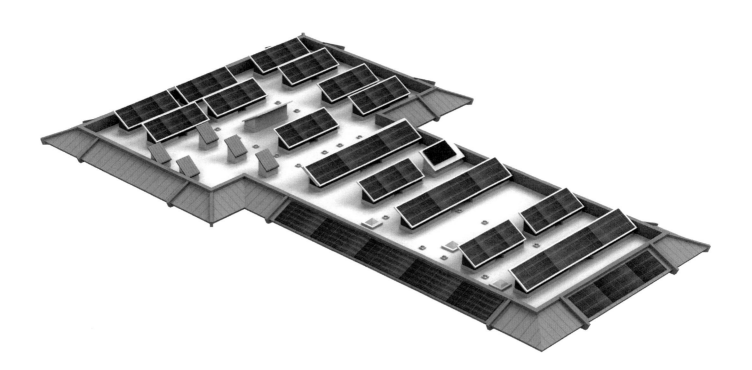

Illustration by Paiching Wei courtesy of the Northern California Sound and Communications NECA-IBEW LMCC

Energy Design Analysis and Energy Performance:
Modeling versus Post-Occupancy Measurements

Energy Use — Modeling

Energy modeling was used extensively during the design phase to evaluate whole building energy performance and to do parametric studies of the cost effectiveness of low-energy design alternatives. Whole building modeling was carried out using the eQuest program, which showed for the final design a total energy use of 237,500 kWh per year, or an EUI of 18.0 kBtu/sq. ft. per year.

Since natural ventilation is a principal strategy to reduce energy use and needed to be included in the energy use estimate, the design team used CFD analysis in and around the 3-D model of the building, combined with the temperature data contained in the weather file, to evaluate when natural ventilation and night flushing could replace normally mechanical cooling. Through these meticulous calculations, the modelers determined that the annual reduction in cooling load seen by the mechanical system would be 16%. This factor was then used directly to reduce the cooling load results from the eQuest energy model in order to simulate the effect of natural ventilation. The accompanying charts on the energy modeling results incorporate this reduction factor.

Energy Use — Actual Measurement and Comparison to Modeling Results

The *master system integrator* reports the measured performance results for the second year of the building's operation (July 2014 — June 2015) as shown in the accompanying charts. The second year is reported since commissioning was completed at this point and the operational characteristics had been established. The total energy used by the building in this year was 215,300 kWh, or an EUI = 16.3 kBtu/sq. ft. per year. This total is approximately 10% less than that indicated by the energy modeling.

Metering on the building does not correspond exactly to the energy categories of the modeling results. The charts showing measured results therefore combine heating, cooling, pump energy and ventilation energy (fans) into the single category of "mechanical". Another difference is that the energy modeling input assumed that the building would be closed in June and July, since there would be no classes during this period, thus showing little consumption in those months. Not surprisingly, the building is now open for other uses in that time period. In spite of this added functional use of the building, the actual energy consumption is still less than the modeled total. The measured data shows a much lower fraction of energy use going to the plug loads, which likely explains the lower overall measured annual energy consumption despite year-round activities at the facility.

As a further note, the solar thermal system was not metered as part of the overall energy use monitoring system to determine the non-renewable energy offset by this system. Electric energy used for its pumps and backup heating is included in the "mechanical" energy total, however.

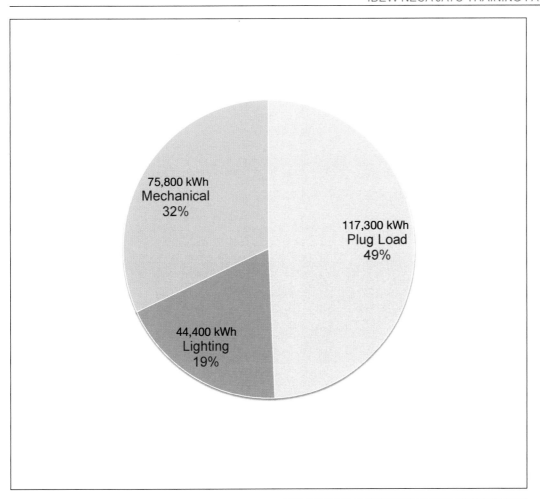

Modeled Energy Use
(Annual)

237,500 kWh per Year
Modeled EUI = 18.0

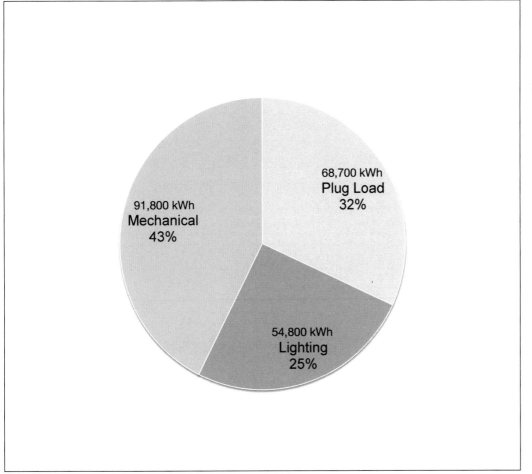

Measured Energy Use
(July 2014 - June 2015)

215,300 kWh per Year
Actual EUI = 16.3

"Mechanical" =
Heating, Cooling, Pumps,
Ventilaton & DHW Backup

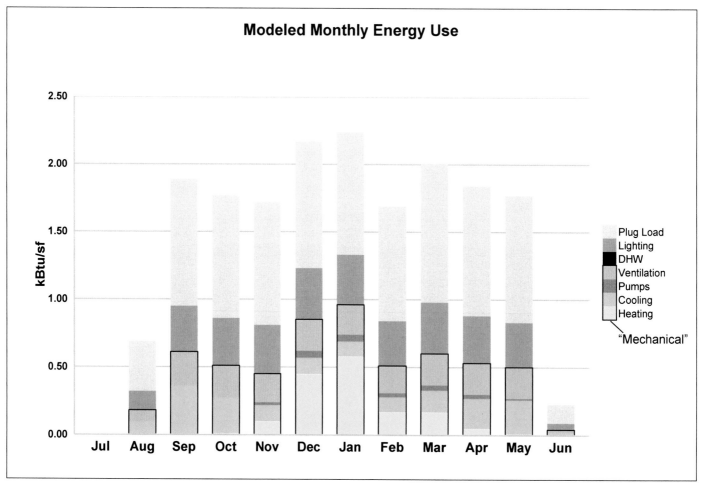

Modeled Monthly Energy Use

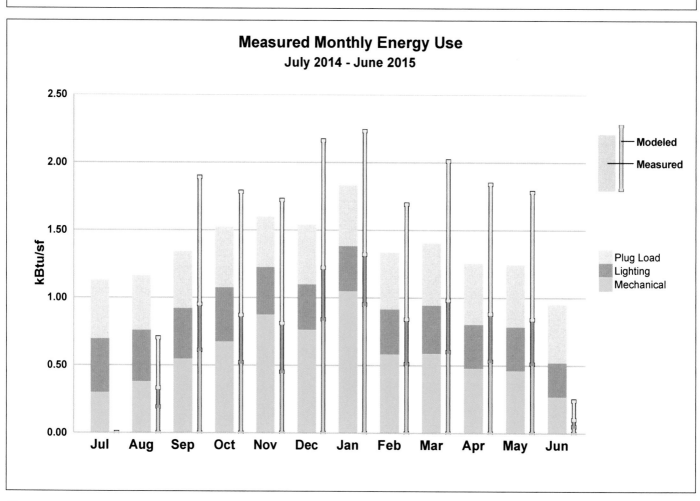

Measured Monthly Energy Use
July 2014 - June 2015

Energy Production versus Energy Use: Zero Net Energy

The measurements recorded during the year of operation from July 2014 to June 2015 indicate that the building is performing at roughly 25% better than ZNE, a strong "net positive" performance. See the accompanying chart (below) showing net monthly energy production versus the energy used monthly by the building.

The chart also shows the relative contribution of each of the three on-site renewable electric energy systems. As noted, the wind turbines are not providing any significant power. The inverter for the Tracking Solar Tree® developed a maintenance issue in the spring of 2015 and the system had to be taken offline; normally, its contribution appears to be 5% - 8% of the total production. The production by the standard fixed PV panel system is providing more than enough power to offset the annual building demand.

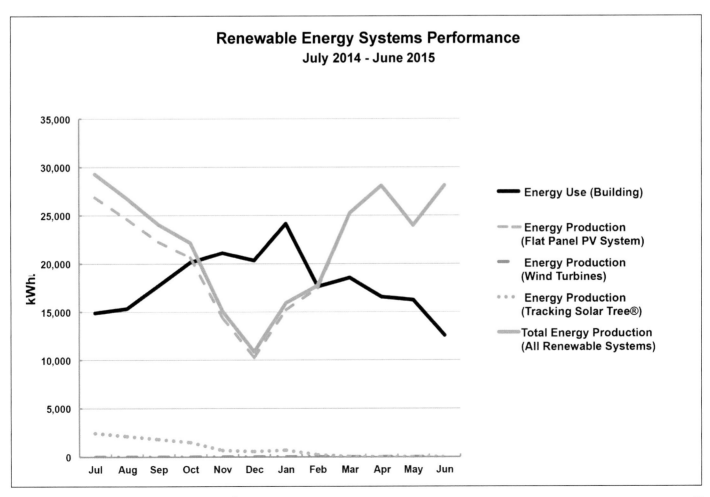

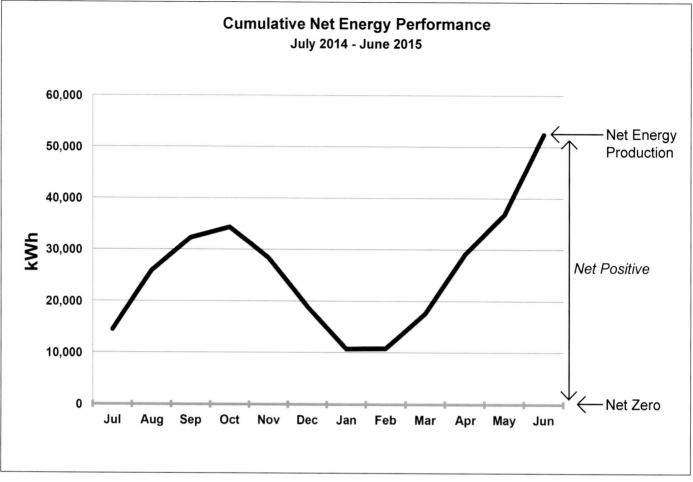

Cumulative Net Energy Performance
July 2014 - June 2015

The chart above showing *Cumulative Energy Balance* over the course of the year also illustrates the *net positive* energy performance. Since the chart begins in July 2014, the curve goes up at first since the net production is positive in the summer months. The curve then turns and goes down through the winter months as the solar energy production is poor, turning up again as the sunny spring season in this location begins in late February.

Post Occupancy: Observations and Conclusions

The renovated building is performing at ZNE or better at the conclusion of a design process that incorporated practical cost criteria with innovative design strategies. The project illustrates that even when cost considerations and practical constraints common to standard renovation projects direct design decisions, there remain effective design strategies that can be used to achieve a ZNE performance.

Post Occupancy: Controls and Monitoring

Engaging a *master system integrator* during design and continuing through the early operation of the facility has proven to have enormous benefit for the owner of this building. The sequence of operations as defined is part of the building's routine function, system monitoring is carried out without difficulty and recording of measured performance data has been correct and readily accessible. This type of seamless operation is a measure of the success of all ZNE buildings and this one in particular.

Post Occupancy: HVAC and Commissioning

Natural ventilation and HVAC system operation have largely conformed to the design intent. Adjustments were made after occupancy on the operation of both HVAC and lighting for rooms that transition from unoccupied to occupied use. It was found that improved operation resulted by setting the classroom spaces to *manual-on* control rather than *occupancy-sensed auto-off* when someone enters the room. Users frequently entered these general-use rooms for very short periods and automatic startup of the systems resulted in excessive operation time. Manual control eliminated these periods of operation that are essentially unnecessary and not desired by the intermittent user.

The window actuator for the openable ventilating windows proved to be excessively noisy. Operation was changed from several setpoints of openness to one or two, as well as adjusting every half hour rather than more frequently, in order to minimize the disruption caused by the noisy actuators.

Post Occupancy: Lighting

Simple motion detectors using ultrasound technology were found to react to the automatic opening of the ventilating windows as well as outside noise when the windows were open. Infrared motion sensors were added to correct such signals if the space was not actually being used.

Post Occupancy: On-Site Renewable Energy Systems

Because the height of the wind turbines is low, their functionality and operation is compromised by turbulence that occurs naturally near the ground and as influenced by the building and its roof monitor structures. The benefit of this system remains limited to its educational value for the students as well as for the symbolism and branding of the *Zero Net Energy Center*, as the building has been named by its owner organization.

The Tracking Solar Tree® essentially has the same limited but important value because of its small contribution to the renewable energy supply compared to the flat-plate PV arrays, its initial cost per installed watt and the maintenance issue associated with its inverter. While this tracking solar equipment collects more energy per unit area of collector, it is still not as cost effective as the simple fixed flat-plate system. It is interesting to note that these two renewable energy systems were chosen in part for educational reasons and, even though they are not cost effective with regard to energy production, the project is still net positive in its energy performance.

Post Occupancy: Occupant Behavior

Like many new ZNE buildings, building users show exemplary consciousness of the vision and goals for the facility's low-energy design. Users take ownership of the building's performance and contribute to a higher level of performance than design analyses indicate as a reasonable target. Also common to many first-time ZNE projects, both client and design team strongly publicize the project and seek to promulgate the information among peer organizations.

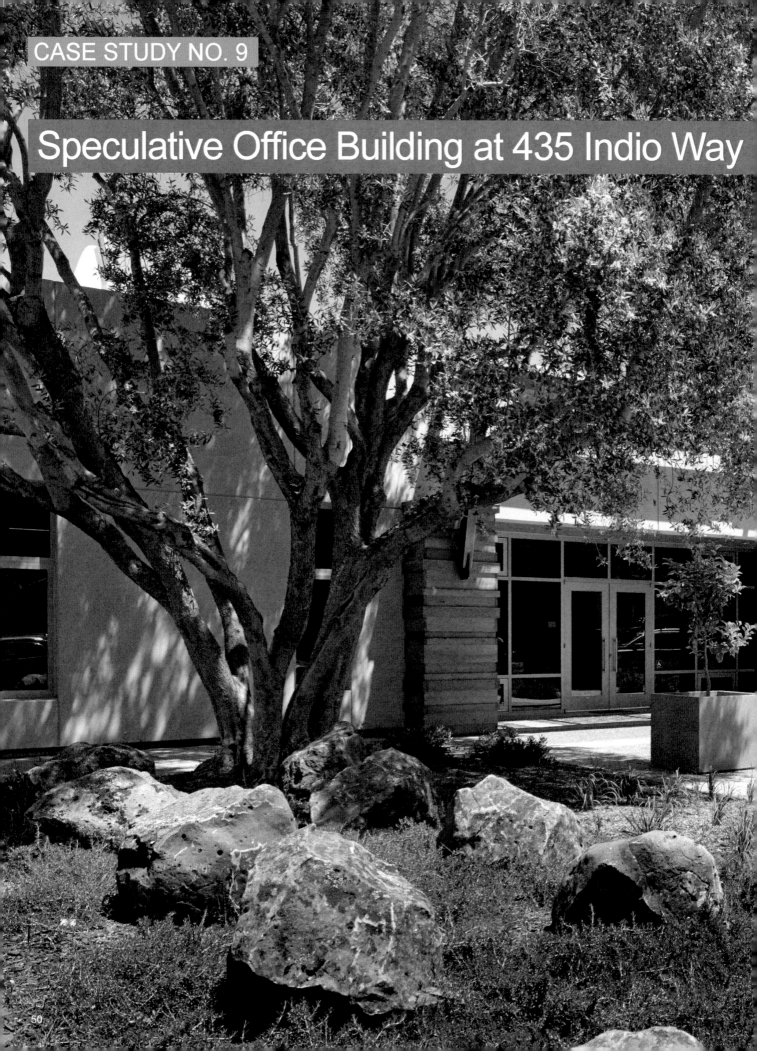

Speculative Office Building at 435 Indio Way

PHOTO: BRUCE DAMONTE

Speculative Office Building at 435 Indio Way
Case Study No. 9

Data Summary

Building Type: Office
Location: Sunnyvale, CA
Gross Floor Area: 31,759 gsf
Occupied: May 2014
Energy Modeling Software:
EnergyPlus 7.2

Modeled EUI (Site):
21.2 kBtu/sf-year

Measured EUI (Site):
13.5 kBtu/sf-year (Oct 2014 —
Sept 2015)

**On-Site Renewable Energy
System Installed:**
113.2 kW (DC) Solar PV

**Measured On-Site Energy
Production:**
266,000 kWh/year
28.6 kBtu/sf-year (Oct 2014 —
Sept 2015)

**Measured Solar Thermal
Production:**
500 kWh/year
0.1 kBtu/sf-year (May 2014 —
June 2015)

Client/Developer
Sharp Development Company

Owner
Huettig & Schromm, Inc.

Design Team
Architect: RMW Architects, San
Jose, CA
Structural Engineer: SEI (Structural Engineers Inc)
Mechanical/Electrical Engineer:
Integral Group, Oakland, CA
Lighting Design: Integral Group,
Oakland, CA
Master System Integrator:
Intertie Automation

General Contractor
Hillhouse Construction Company

Case Study No. 9, the *Speculative Office Building at 435 Indio Way* in Sunnyvale, California, is the third renovation project in the set of successful zero-net-energy case study buildings documented in this Volume 2. Like Case Study No. 8, the IBEW-NECA JATC Training Center, this project is also the renovation of an existing one-story tilt-up concrete building in a suburban office park and therefore very interesting to compare[1]. These two buildings are essentially of the same vintage and construction, and are located in similar microclimate areas, thus providing the opportunity to compare design approach and the basis of decision-making.

The principal differences between the two case study buildings are programmatic use—education versus general office use—and the types of financial criteria established for decision-making about low-energy design features and systems.

As noted in Case Study No. 8, every such design feature for that project was individually evaluated on a life-cycle cost basis, with the underlying accepted objective that the building would be designed for ZNE. Features with relatively high life cycle cost were not accepted; for example, even wall insulation was not selected because of the relatively low impact on energy savings combined with the relatively high cost of retrofit installation.

For Case Study No. 9, on the other hand, the financial criteria were strict but general: the total *return on investment* for the ZNE design as a whole was required to be greater than that of a code-minimum building design. The ZNE design simply had to be a better financial investment than a code-minimum building by the standard metrics of real estate development.

The developer and owners of the building wished to develop a ZNE prototype design for a common project-type in their real estate market, the concrete tilt-up in an office park, and to test the market with it. They believed (and wanted to confirm) that the ZNE design could be shown to produce just as much or even more profit when compared with a code-minimum design despite potentially higher first cost for the ZNE design. Savings and added value in other financial areas due to the ZNE design would theoretically make up any difference in first cost or would even increase the profitability bottom line.

Because of the importance of this concept of financial investment in ZNE design, details of the financial comparisons done by the developer for this building are discussed in a special sidebar in this particular case study.

All three of these case studies in Volume 2 (Nos. 7, 8 and 9) indicate that renovation projects for buildings of this type and in comparable locations are highly feasible candidates for zero net energy performance under typical types of financial constraints.

Background

The approximately 30,000 sq. ft., one-story building, built in the 1970's when energy standards were just being launched in California, is owned by Huettig & Schromm, Inc., a property management company in Palo Alto. The partners were particularly interested in renovating the building so that it would be *zero net energy* and they involved Sharp Development Company to realize that objective. Both parties believed that there was an exceptional market for this type of building space in their geographic area and they wished to test this idea.

---

[1] See also Case Study No. 3, *IDeAs Office Building*, in Volume 1 of *Zero Net Energy Case Study Buildings*. This project was also a renovation of a one-story tilt-up concrete building in a suburban setting, though of a much smaller size. Additional comparisons among these renovation projects are instructive.

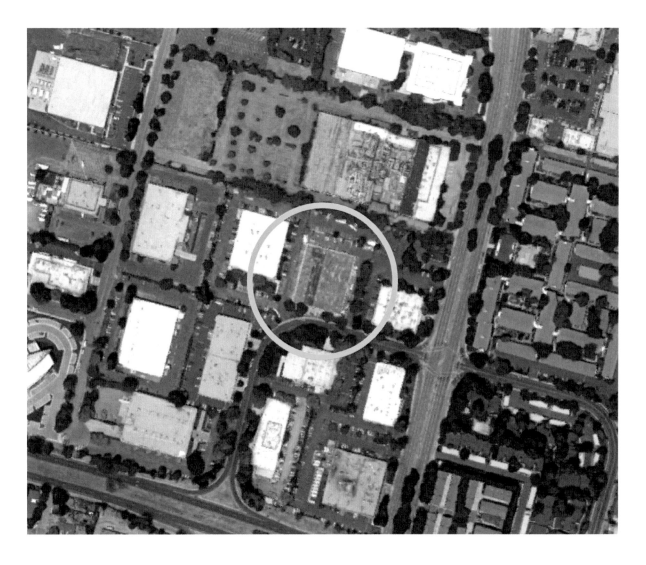

Speculative Office Building at 435 Indio Way: General Vicinity Plan

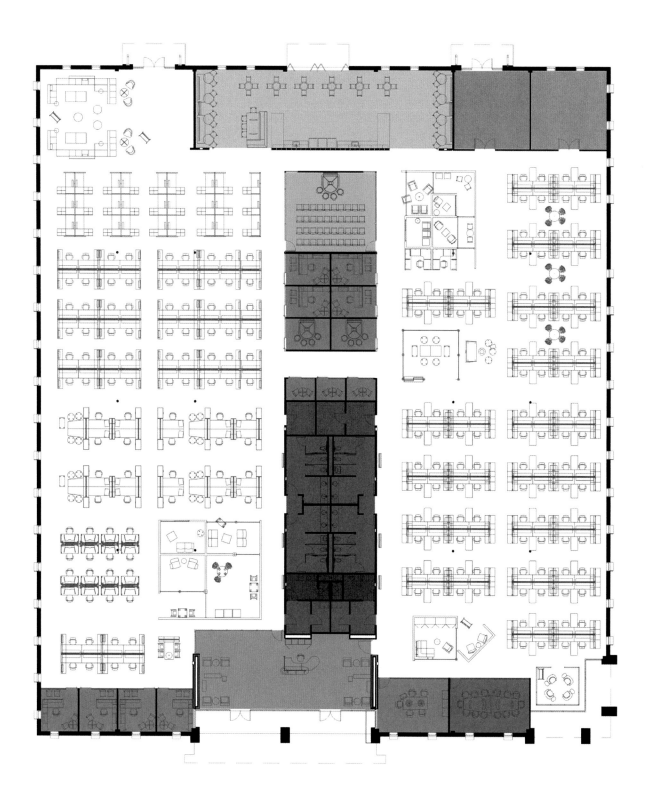

Speculative Office Building at 435 Indio Way: Floor Plan

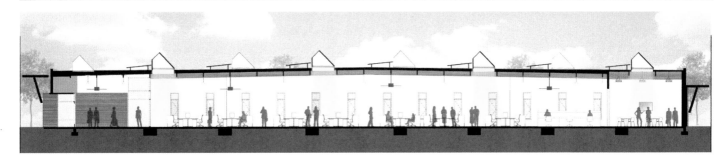

The project team was largely assembled over time, with Sharp engaging the engineering team and the general contractor initially, followed by the design architect. Project delivery was established as design-build, with strong contractor involvement in engineering and architectural decisions.

The project team anticipated that, because of the passive design approach that was initially taken (passive ventilation and use of the thermal mass for pre-cooling), a key to success in ZNE performance would be a seamlessly operating set of control systems. For that reason, a master system integrator was added to the team in the design phase to work with the engineering team with regard to the *sequence of operations* for coordination of all building systems.

Design Process and Low Energy Design Strategies

The design process was driven by two principal directives: the resulting renovation must be a ZNE-performing building and, at the same time, the developed project must be a more profitable investment than a code-minimum renovation of the same building would be.

To accomplish this, the project team evaluated the effect of every energy-related design decision on the overall performance and measured this total against the overriding financial directive. Hard bids of both the ZNE alternative and the code-minimum alternative were obtained and put into the financial pro forma analysis. The bottom-line profitability of both alternatives was evaluated throughout the process, ultimately confirming that the ZNE design in fact had a better bottom line (higher profitability) for this project.

See the *Profitability Sidebar* on the next page for a summary of the methodology and outcome of this financial analysis.

Planning Concept and General Design Considerations

With this project, the owners and developer wanted to develop a more holistic approach to the integrated design of ZNE features and systems. They recognized that many building features provide benefits—even financial benefits—that cannot be easily quantified but have been measured in other ways. For example, office space with daylighting and a connection to nature has been shown to be associated with higher productivity among building users, as well as simply being more desirable space among potential tenants who recognize this.

With this in mind, the owners used this approach to select the mix of design features and systems for the ZNE design, while keeping a close watch on its profitability bottom line in comparison to the code-minimum building.

(Left) View of the original 1970s building before renovation. (Photo courtesy of RMW Architects).

Sidebar: Profitability

The building featured in Case Study No. 9 is regarded by its owners as primarily a financial investment, not a R&D project and not necessarily a demonstration project for highly sustainable ZNE buildings. With this prime directive in mind, they could have developed the property with a *business-as-usual* (BAU) approach—a code-minimum building with the lowest first cost possible. They strongly suspected, however, that in their market and for this type of risk investment, the ZNE design approach would actually prove to be *more* profitable according to the standard financial analysis used by developers. This proved to be a correct assessment in the end, as the summary analysis in this Sidebar shows.

The owners used a 7.5% "cap rate"[1]. For the building, the income stream divided by the cap rate equals the *value* of this investment. The market in this type of real estate was 5.5% - 6% at the time, so setting a higher standard for the performance of the investment was a conservative strategy and a hedge against any changes in the market before leasing could start.

The tabulation shown below shows the final comparison of the code-minimum (BAU) building design with the ZNE building design. The full financial spreadsheet was maintained and updated throughout the design/construction/leasing period. Some of the financial advantages (the *value proposition*) of the ZNE building, contributing to the profitability *bottom line* beyond first cost considerations are:

- The operating and maintenance cost is less for the ZNE building because of its simpler and smaller systems.
- The reserve requirement is lower, providing additional savings, because of the smaller and simpler HVAC system and the lower cost for *tenant improvements* upon turnover.
- Earlier lease-up was expected because of the appeal to tenants of occupying a ZNE building with higher indoor air quality. This was proven, as the building leased 15 months faster than the market average and the owners received 15 months of rent for the period that would normally be lease-up time.
- For the same reasons, the rental income is higher than the *market comparables* and the *churn rate* (tenant changes and "down time") is lower, boosting cash flow.

The numbers show that if the investor is going to sell the property soon after construction ("build to sell"), the ZNE building is more profitable even using the higher cap rate because of the increased value, even though the project cost is higher (in this case by $49.84/sq. ft.). If the investor is going to hold the property, the ZNE building is even more profitable because of the higher cash flow, which pays off the additional project cost in just a few years, while the added value of the property is still in place.

Cost Information	Code-Minimum (BAU)	Sustainable [2] ZNE Building	Difference	Per Sq. Ft.
Total A & E Cost	$260,800	$337,700	($76,900)	
Total Hard Cost	$2,865,944	$4,042,458	($1,176,514)	
Total Soft Cost	$426,550	$410,629	$15,921	
Solar Photovoltaic System Cost	$0	$345,228	($345,228)	
A **Total Cost**	**$3,553,294**	**$5,136,015**	**($1,582,721)**	($49.84)

Income Information / Valuation				
Annual rent net of operating expenses	$847,194	$1,086,848	$239,654	
B Value of Rent Differential at 7.5% cap rate			$3,195,387	$100.61
C Rent during first 18 mos. after completion	$0	$724,500	$724,500	$22.81
Net Additional Value if sold in 18 mos. (A+B+C)			$2,337,166	$73.59
PG&E and Govt. Rebates	$0	$298,764	$298,764	$9.41
Additional Value if include rebates			$2,635,930	$83.00

Cash Flow				
Additional Cost			($1,582,721)	($49.84)
Less Early Lease-up			$724,500	$22.81
Net additional Cost				($27.02)
Net Cash Flow after Debt Service	$585,350	$708,373	$123,023	$3.87
Years to amortize with cash flow			6.98	

Rental Income Differential				NNN Rent [3]
Operating Expenses	$280,220	$185,540	$94,680	$0.25
TI Replacement Reserves	$62,866	$47,638	$15,228	$0.04
Additional 326 SF of space	$0	$15,114	$15,114	$0.04
Premium over market rent & operating expenses	$0	$114,632	$114,632	$0.30
Total Equivalent Increase in NNN Rental Income			**$239,654**	**$0.63**

[2] These cost numbers are actually based on hard bids obtained for both the Code-Minimum building and the ZNE building.

[3] "NNN", a *triple net lease*, is a lease agreement where the tenant pays all real estate taxes, building insurance and maintenance in addition to rent and utilities. Note that the lease agreement for the ZNE building is actually a *Full Service* lease so that the owner could capture the value of the utility cost savings created by the initial investment in the ZNE building.

The higher profitability for the ZNE building is confirmed by the analysis and the experience of the first year of operation. The owners are now pursuing similar projects, with even better numbers for early lease-up and rental income.

---

[1] The "cap rate" is the rate of return that an investor wants to receive in the marketplace with this type of "risk profile". The rate of return determines the investment's value.

An example is the decision to use electrochromic or *dynamic glass*[2] instead of insulated glass combined with exterior shades or interior blinds. Athough electrochromic glass outperforms the blinds/shading solution because of its fine-tuned operation with respect to solar impact, this fact alone would not have led to its selection based only on energy savings because of the premium initial cost. However, this product provides a greater connection to the outdoors during the day due to its operating characteristics and it was deemed to have an intrinsic appeal to user-tenants in this geographic market area. Because of these additional benefits, the holistic process showed that the overall ZNE design including the electrochromic glass would still be more profitable than the code-minimum design.

Replacement windows using electrochromic glazing.

The project team chose a *passive* approach for its low-energy design concept. Even though the site is in a relatively warm microclimate where buildings can have a significant cooling load in the warm months, the night temperatures during that time fall into a range where "free cooling" can be used to pre-cool the large thermal mass of concrete walls. Also, for a good part of the year, natural ventilation near the exterior walls can provide cooling air during the day. The design strategies for the building envelope and the HVAC system, therefore, are aimed at optimizing the use of these aspects of building and microclimate in a passive way.

Building Envelope

The existing building was a standard one-story concrete tilt-up construction with uninsulated walls and minimally insulated roof. As with Case Study No, 8, the lightweight roof structure would have to be strengthened to support a new solar photovoltaic system; because of the daylighting design solution in this case (see below), the roof structural strengthening had to be done.

The passive design concept for the building called for insulating the exterior walls on the outside surfaces so that the mass of the concrete was available for heat exchange with the cool night air. At the same time, the BMS (Building Management System) controls the building fans to operate at night if the outdoor air temperature is low enough and if a cooling load is anticipated for the following day.

The team settled on 5-5/8" thick polystyrene retrofitted to the exterior wall surface. EIFS (Exterior Insulation Finishing System) was used to provide a finish over the thick layer of insulation. There is no foundation insulation primarily for cost reasons; the polystyrene ends at the level of the concrete floor slab. The concrete floor slab and the layer of ground beneath it act as additional thermal storage mass and, for this reason, the use of carpet is discouraged as part of tenant improvements[3].

All existing single glazed windows were replaced by double-glazing. The electrochromic glass was used on all but the north side of the building, where a lightly tinted low-e insulated glass was used. Since many of the windows were converted to openable casement windows, a method had to be developed for using the electrochromic glass units in the openable sash, i.e., a method to ensure that the electric wiring connection functioned flawlessly for the life of the windows. This issue was one of many that was successfully researched and solved by the contractor.

Retrofitted polystyrene insulation at exterior wall surfaces.

[2] *Dynamic glass* or electrochromic glass is electronically tintable glass units, setting solar heat gain and light transmission of the glass at a pre-programmed level or through instant control via portable device. A light sensor reading outside the glass panel is compared to the desired interior condition; the glass system then sets the tint based on the preferred interior light condition for minimal glare and best daylight levels. The glass is therefore tuned to the space.
[3] Per the terms of the lease agreement, the tenant must pay for any energy charges in excess of the ZNE baseline.

Daylighting and Electric Lighting

Daylighting of the entire space is accomplished using an array of a uniquely designed skylight, which was originally conceived for a colder climate application. The idea is to minimize heat loss and gain through the glazing while producing the same amount of daylight normally available through north-facing glazing in roof monitors, a traditional method of daylighting through the roof. (See Case Study No. 8.)

This is accomplished by facing the glazing toward the south rather than the north, thereby collecting a greater intensity of solar energy per unit area of glazing. (See the illustration on the facing page.) The amount of glazing, and therefore the amount of structure carrying the skylights, can be much less in size and material for the same amount of captured daylight. The design of the skylight structure itself, however, must be carefully shaped in the roof and the ceiling below it in order to diffuse the light appropriately and to avoid creating counter-productive glare conditions. To accomplish this, the glazing must be covered with a light-diffusing film, preventing any view of the sky but overcoming the inevitable glare that would result with clear glass.

Studies were undertaken to determine the size of the glazed opening and the skylight spacing, as well as the tilt of the skylight glazing toward the south, in order to optimize the level of daylight under clear sky conditions during most of the year from morning through the afternoon hours. The objective was to arrive at the best set of design parameters so that electric lighting would

9 sq ft North Facing Clerestory

3 sq ft South Facing Skylight

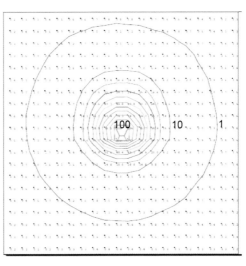

(Left) Sample study results: Iso-illuminance curves n footcandles at the floor level for the two orientations of the glazing. (Diagram courtesy of Integral Group).

40' x 40' area - average footcandles at Dec 21 noon:

North Clerestory - 0.35 fc/s.f.   South Skylight – 2.15 fc/s.f.

~ 6 : 1 ratio

PHOTO: BRUCE DAMONTE

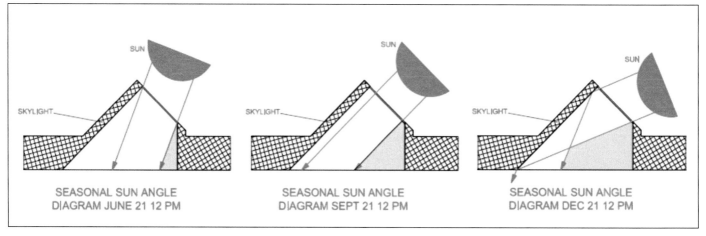

SEASONAL SUN ANGLE
DIAGRAM JUNE 21 12 PM

SEASONAL SUN ANGLE
DIAGRAM SEPT 21 12 PM

SEASONAL SUN ANGLE
DIAGRAM DEC 21 12 PM

(Above) View directly up into skylight aperture. (Photo courtesy of Integral Group.)

not be needed at any time under these conditions. The daylight studies showed, for example, that the glazing should be sloped at an angle perpendicular to the solar altitude at 12 noon at the equinox (March 21 and September 21). See the illustration above. (Diagram courtesty of Integral Group.)

The skylight structures are constructed of fiberglass and can be dropped into roof openings as required to get a generally even distribution of daylight across the floor below. Measurements taken under clear sky conditions showed a light level of 19 footcandles at 30" above the floor plane (workstation height). This is a good general lighting level and the expectation is that this light level would be augmented by local task lighting by the tenant, as needed at workstations.

Suspended light fixtures using LED light sources are placed farther apart than normal, with the idea that they simply replace the daylight levels when daylight is not available in a typical ambient/task type of lighting design approach. The LED lights are dimmable in response to daylight availability and are additionally controlled by motion and infrared sensors.

PHOTO: BRUCE DAMONTE

61

PHOTO: BRUCE DAMONTE

Natural Ventilation

Windows are openable at the perimeter of the building, including all glazing using the electro-chromic glass. The skylights are automatically opened by actuators as part of the "night flushing" of the building for pre-cooling during the warm months. The ground level windows are also opened at night automatically during the night flushing operation, but the amount of opening is limited to maintain security; the security alarm system is designed to further protect against unauthorized entry.

As part of the passive systems design for the building, larger spaces requiring fresh air, such as large conference rooms, are prescribed to be located at the perimeter of the space so that they can be passively ventilated and cooled. This information is provided to tenants as part of the "driver's manual" for the building and an explanation of the *passive systems* used in the building to achieve ZNE performance.

Heating, Ventilating and Cooling Systems

The HVAC system consists of distributed air-source heat pump units (two units at 11 tons each). These units are basically back-up heating and cooling for the passive systems of the building. They are sized for large group events; as a result, they operate at partial loads under normal conditions, an efficient mode of operation.

If private offices are built as part of the tenant improvements, individual comfort control is achieved by using *Therma-fusers™* [4] at each of the private offices. This device eliminates the need for a separate system for these office spaces.

Like most ZNE buildings, the design also includes large ceiling-mounted room fans to create air movement for comfort, thereby allowing a higher cooling temperature setpoint for the HVAC system. The high ceilings in buildings of this type lend themselves to this particular energy-saving strategy.

The basic sequence of operations is the *mixed-mode* type. When outdoor temperatures are moderate and can be used for cooling, windows and skylights open for natural ventilation. If the outdoor temperature rises, the large ceiling fans are engaged. For higher outdoor temperatures still, the windows and skylights close automatically and the air-conditioning units operate to cool the spaces.

Domestic Hot Water

The building utilizes a standard solar thermal hot water system with storage and electric resistance backup for domestic hot water (DHW).

Plug Loads

The information given to tenants at the time of leasing includes recommendations for energy-efficient (Energy Star®) equipment. Installed circuit metering on tenant space provides feedback and information to tenants about their plug load use.

---

[4] *Therma-Fusers™* are ceiling air diffusers operating as an integrated Variable Air Volume (VAV) zone of temperature control. These diffusers include a thermostat, modulating damper and diffuser in a single package.

PHOTO: BRUCE DAMONTE

Master System Integration and Control Systems

This case study building benefited from the experience with ZNE buildings over the past several years and the evolving understanding in the industry about the importance of master system integration for the various control systems used in "smart buildings" such as ZNE performers. The owner contracted with a building controls ("Building OS") software company[5] during the design phase to advise on the overall controls for this case study building. Understanding the state of the controls industry at the time, the software company hired an experienced independent *master system integrator*[6] to advise on how to proceed.

The arrangement evolved so that the *integrator* became a member of the design-build team, working with the designers and in the field to develop an *omni-controller* that functioned smoothly according to the defined *sequence of operations* for all passive system controls (sensors, window and skylight actuators, room fans, etc.) as well as the standard HVAC system controls. After the commissioning was completed, the integrator was engaged under a facilities maintenance contract by the owner to monitor the omni-controller and the connected systems, to ensure continued quality performance.

The integrator based the design of the omni-controller on a residential version of an building industry control system[7] and implemented a BACnet[8] communications protocol with it so that the system could communicate with the HVAC system, for which BACnet is standard.

The design of the omni-controller also included another innovation: the *sequence of operations* for the passive systems requires that a signal be sent to the actuators of windows and skylights for a range of operation. The integrator developed communication software for both wired and wireless connection to the microprocessors of the actuators. For the wired applications, a *universal powerline bus (UPB)*[9] was used. For the wireless applications, the integrator used *ZigBee*[10]. The actuators specified did not allow partial opening set points, but only "open", "close" and "stop", so the integrator attached a timer and tuned the system so that the actuators could stop at various degrees of openness.

Lighting controls are left as a stand-alone system, built into the light fixture system as part of the manufactured design[11]. The metering of electric energy use was also initially left as a stand-alone system, connected to the cloud-based data recording system and the building's energy dashboard. However, this was changed after ten months of occupancy to a connection with the omni-controller so that the integrator could have access to the building performance data as part of the overall monitoring of the building systems. (See *Post Occupancy: Observations and Conclusions*, below.)

---

[5] *Lucid*, https://lucidconnects.com/

[6] *Intertie Automation*, San Francisco, CA

[7] *Leviton*, http://www.leviton.com/OA_HTML/SectionDisplay.jsp?section=37575&minisite=10251

[8] *BACnet* is a communications protocol for building automation and control networks. It is an ASHRAE, ANSI, and ISO 16484-5 standard protocol.

[9] *Universal Powerline Bus (UPB)* is a communication protocol for sending digital signals between devices using electric power line wiring for signal and control.

[10] *Zigbee* is an IEEE 802.15.4-based specification for a suite of communication protocols used to create local area wireless networks of very low power. "ZigBee is the only open, global wireless standard to provide the foundation for the *Internet of Things* by enabling simple and smart objects to work together...", from http://www.zigbee.org/.

[11] *Enlighted Inc.*, http://www.enlightedinc.com/

Commissioning

Commissioning was managed and carried out by the general contractor and design-build team, as well as by the master system integrator with the extensive work on the omni-control system and the continuing supervision of operations during the early occupancy period.

Renewable On-Site Energy Supply

The building uses a standard flat-panel solar photovoltaic system as its on-site renewable energy supply. Roof area is more than adequate for the size of the system (113 kW) needed to offset the annual energy consumption by the building energy systems, even with the requirement to avoid shading the south-facing skylight glazing.

Energy Design Analysis and Energy Performance:
Modeling versus Post-Occupancy Measurements

Energy Use — Modeling

Energy modeling was carried out during the design phases using *EnergyPlus v7.2*. The modeling provided whole building energy use, allowing the team to size the solar photovoltaic system needed for ZNE performance. It was also used for parametric studies to evaluate energy savings resulting from different designs, in particular for the passive systems. The final design model yielded a total annual energy use of 197,000 kWh, or an EUI of 21.2 kBtu/sf per year.

Temperature sensors placed at the concrete floor slab have indicated that the energy model underestimates heat absorption by the mass and over-estimates the release of heat from the mass. In future projects, energy modelers will note this difference in the output reporting.

Energy Use — Actual Measurement and Comparison to Modeling Results

Energy use data was separately recorded with the cloud-based monitoring system that also communicated this information to the energy dashboard. The accompanying charts show the energy-use performance over the one-year period from October 2014 through the same month in 2015. The total energy used by the building in this year was 125,500 kWh, or an EUI = 13.5 kBtu/sf per year. This total is approximately 35% less than that indicated by the energy modeling, which uses a "standard" weather file for the location.

This lower-than-expected energy use is likely due to the sunnier winter in a California drought year as well as the tenant's attention to energy-efficient use of the building, particularly the free-cooling available in the relatively mild climate. (The building was fully occupied in the year that the energy use data was collected.) Another factor may have been the better overall performance of the concrete floor for passive cooling compared to the calculations of the energy model.

The charts on the following pages summarize the modeled performance and the actual performance of the building in its first year of occupancy. This first year included about three months of non-occupancy by the tenant that now occupies the entire building.

Modeled Energy Use
(Annual)

197,000 kWh/year
Modeled EUI =21.2

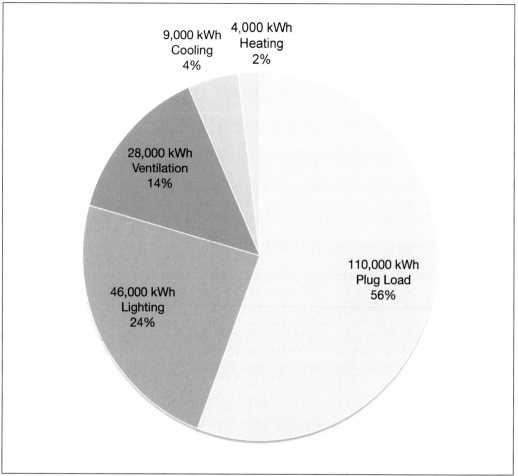

Measured Energy Use
Oct 2014 - Sep 2015

125,500 kWh/year
Measured EUI = 13.5

"Mechanical" =
Heating, Cooling & Ventilation

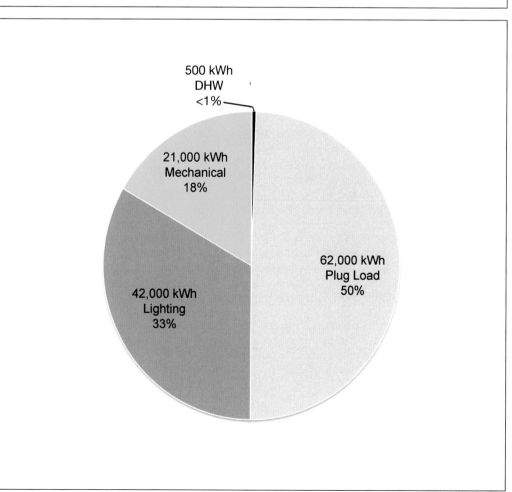

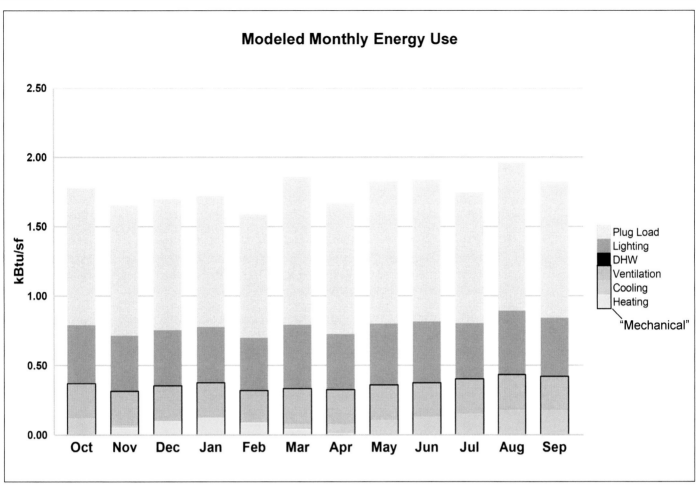

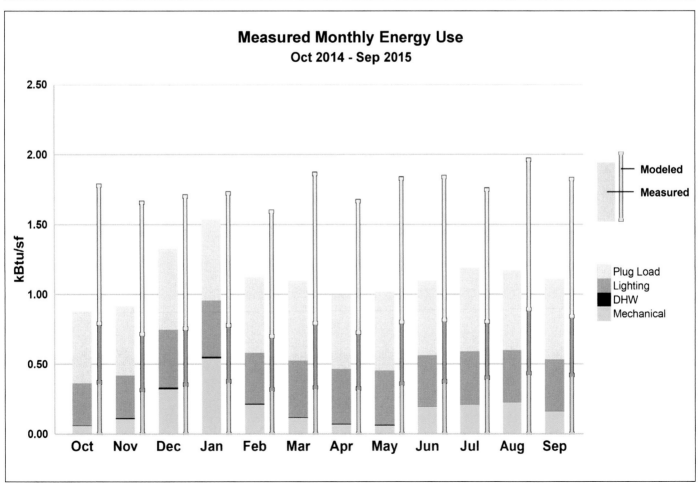

Energy Production versus Energy Use: Zero Net Energy

As noted above, after ten months of building operation the integrator modified the design of the omni-controller to collect the metered data being communicated to the cloud-based monitoring system connected to the energy dashboard. A review of all monitored data over that period revealed that one of the inverters was failing to report energy production data; there was no record for that entire period. A correction to the equipment was made and data collection by the one inverter was re-started. Since that time, the integrator has been regularly monitoring proper energy production data from the entire system.

Net energy metering records for the building were available from the utility, so the energy production charts for this case study building are based on the combination of the utility's net-metered data and the fully recorded energy consumption data.

See the chart on the facing page for a depiction of this energy production during the first year of operation based on these records, compared with the energy use measurements for the building during the same period. A system shut-down for a period of time in August is clearly visible in the output data.

The *Cumulative Energy Balance* chart for the period 10/2014 – 9/2015 illustrates the net positive performance of the building, with the net total on-site energy balance at the end of that one-year period still positive on the production side.

Post Occupancy: Observations and Conclusions

The project has met both its financial and energy performance goals. As illustrated in the Sidebar discussion of the profitability of this ZNE building versus a code-minimum alternative, the project with its ZNE design is indeed more profitable for this type of investment in this location. Indeed, this prototype for such an approach to developing ZNE buildings has proved to be so successful in this market that the second project by these developers, now in construction, was leased out before construction even started. (The case study building required three months to lease after construction was completed—still within the range of financial parameters required for the ZNE design.) The developer concludes that it may prove to be the case that when the market is soft, ZNE buildings will get leased first.

Consistency of these results over a wider range of building types and market locations may prove to be the case in the future.

Post Occupancy: Controls and Monitoring

The use of UPB (*Universal Powerline Bus*) for omni-controller communication has proved to be very successful with this case study building. All room fans and actuators to windows and skylights use UPD. To work well, it is essential that the system essentially be connected with "clean" power (i.e., electric current without extraneous electrical signals from certain types of electrical equipment on the same circuit). This requires these devices to be connected to the same panel, keeping line "noise" to a minimum.

While the UPB application has proven to be economical and very reliable, BACnet systems are currently not able to use it. This may change as the industry evolves.

Additional improvements during this period include the addition of sensors for CO_2 and VOC content in building air. These sensors are now part of the sensor network (temperature, humid-

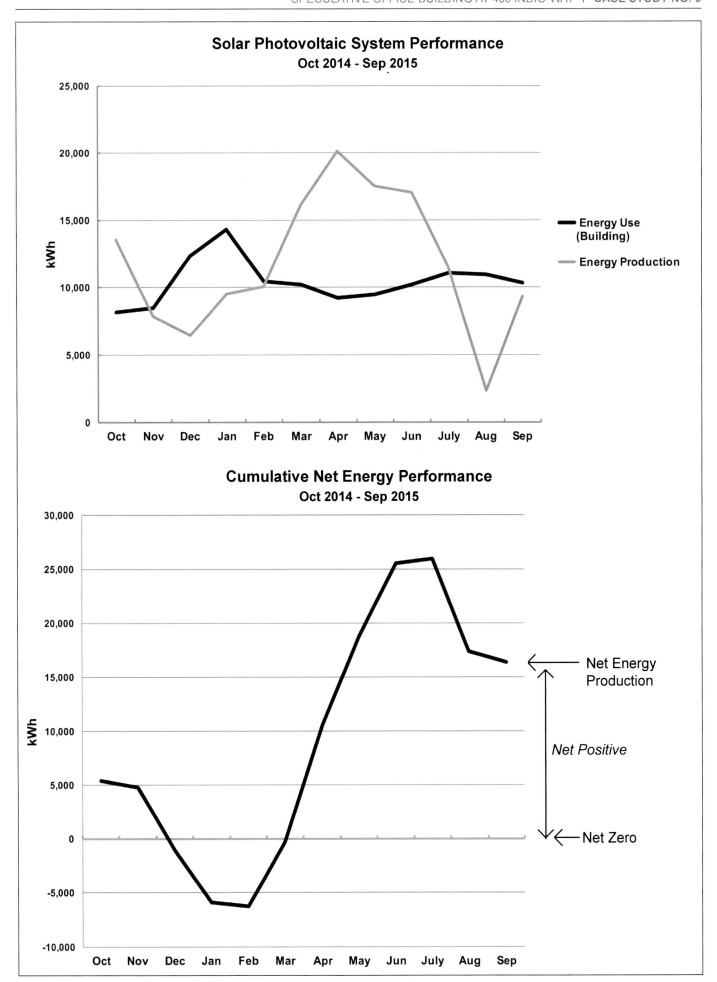

PHOTO: BRUCE DAMONTE

ity and chemical of concern) that is being used to monitor indoor air quality. This is part of the package being offered to prospective tenants who value basic principles of *sustainability* in their office space.

The discovery after ten months of building operation that one of the solar PV inverters was not recording production data indicated the need not only for continued commissioning activity during the early post-occupancy period, but also for assignment of knowledgeable staff to monitor data that is being produced by the system in order to make it actionable.

Post Occupancy: HVAC and Commissioning

The initial tenant in the space decided that its conference rooms should be located at the interior of the building, rather than at the perimeter as prescribed in the building's ZNE passive systems "drivers' manual". (The tenant's reason is to provide full access to the openable windows for staff at workstations.) As a result, outside air for cooling would not ordinarily reach these interior spaces without a separate system. Engineers added transfer ducts so that the cooling air could reach into these conference rooms and provide adequate fresh air and cooling.

As noted, separate commissioning was not required because of the commitment of the design-build team to the success of the ZNE design as well as the engagement of the master system integrator from design through post-occupancy.

Post Occupancy: Lighting

As noted in the discussion of the skylights and lighting design for this case study building, the design provides enough daylight on bright days for general illumination of the office space but ordinarily would be combined with task lighting at the work surface as part of the "ambient/task" approach to lighting design in this building. For this reason, the LED light fixtures are spaced apart to provide the same general level of lighting when daylight is not available.

The tenant, however, has a typical "tech company" environment with computer monitors at simple tables and their staff prefer not to use task lighting at the desks. Rather, they override the electric light fixtures in order to keep them turned on at all times and reduce the perceived variation of daylighting. The combination of the LED lights at wide spacing and the daylight monitors provides a largely even lighting with only a small variation through the day provided by the daylighting.

The tenant reports that for continuous work on computer monitors, discernible light variation actually leads to migraine headaches in some cases and the constant low-level light from the LED fixtures successfully mitigates this effect from the daylight variation. The relatively high efficiency of the LED light sources apparently does not create a significant energy "penalty" for the building's overall performance.

Post Occupancy: Occupant Behavior

The monitoring of the plug loads in tenant space provided an alert to the new tenant that a batch of its equipment was using excessive amounts of energy compared to energy-efficient alternatives. The tenant realized that replacement of their older equipment, which was driving the high energy consumption, would be a cost effective action and developed a plan to do so.

West Berkeley Branch Library

PHOTO: KYLE JEFFERS

75

West Berkeley Branch Library
Case Study No. 10

Data Summary

Building Type: Civic / Library
Location: Berkeley, CA
Gross Floor Area: 9,300 gsf
Occupied: January 2014
Energy Modeling Software:
DesignBuilder v2.1 (updated modeling using v4.5.0.178)

Modeled EUI (Site):
17.5 kBtu/sq.ft.-year
Measured EUI (Site):
23.1 kBtu/sq.ft.-year (2014)

On-Site Renewable Energy System Installed:
52.2 kW (DC) Solar PV
Measured On-Site Energy Production:
75,350 kWh per year
27.7 kBtu/sq.ft.-year (2014)

Owner/Client
City of Berkeley, Berkeley Public Library

Design Team
Architect: Harley Ellis Devereaux, Berkeley Office and Los Angeles, CA
Structural Engineer: Tipping-Mar, Berkeley, CA
Mechanical/Electrical/Plumbing Design Engineer: Timmons Design Engineers, San Francisco, CA
Energy Modeling: GreenWorks Studio, Los Angeles,CA
Lighting Design: Max Pierson, San Francisco, CA
Landscape Architect: John Northmore Roberts & Associates, Berkeley, CA

General Contractor
West Bay Builders, Novato, CA

The *West Berkeley Branch Library* is a model for the basic design process of a ZNE building, particularly for a building in the public sector. The project demonstrates the sequence of typical steps starting in concept design and the timely integration of energy-related design principles with the basic aspects of program, spatial relationships, structure and building form. The design process discussed in this case study also illustrates typical timing of technical studies, including computer modeling, and recommended steps through construction and post-occupancy.

The case study project is also an example of the typical public project financial model as applied to ZNE buildings, as opposed to private owners with their own programs and financial objectives, namely a fixed budget with no additional funds earmarked for ZNE design features or systems. The ZNE design must be achieved using a pre-established fixed budget that is usually based on a code-minimum building.

Public clients typically have a lengthy funding process with fixed construction budgets that are determined well in advance of design and construction. While some design alternatives can be evaluated based on life cycle cost, the bottom line for the total project remains a fixed amount that cannot be exceeded. Conversely, if the project is over budget in mid-design, *value engineering* to reduce cost may consider life cycle cost advantages for some building features or systems, but the sum of all selected cost reductions must result in the project meeting the fixed budget.

Background

After years of studies, grant applications and master planning (2000-2008) to replace the inadequate existing branch library at the project site, the voters of the City of Berkeley passed a library bond measure to fund the construction of this branch library, as well as three other branches within the city. The construction budget was set at $5.5 million for the West Branch in 2008; the budget remained at this amount up to the time of bidding four years later in 2012, without any adjustment for inflation during the protracted design approvals period. The project was planned to follow the typical public process of design-bid-build, resulting in a code-minimum building and any adjustments needed to obtain a LEED-Silver rating.

The design team, however, proposed a more aggressive approach to the client, the Berkeley Public Library, suggesting that the building was an ideal candidate for a ZNE design and that this higher goal could be achieved within the fixed budget allotted to the project. The client agreed to allow the design team to proceed with this approach provided the library program was met in full and the final ZNE design satisfied all budget requirements.

The project approvals process started early in the design phases and included a substantial number of public meetings and commentary, including design review and even a lawsuit. A principal issue was the demolition of the remaining portion of the original 1923 building on the project site, which had received a city designation as a "structure of merit". One of the arguments used against the new ZNE design and in favor of the restoration of this original building was *embodied energy*. The design team was able to show that the extra embodied energy needed for the construction of the ZNE design, including that of the glass solar PV panels, would be equaled by the energy saved in operation after only 1.5 years. The calculation demonstrated that the ZNE building design was by far the low-energy and low-carbon alternative.

The general interest in the community for constructing a ZNE public building, combined with library operation factors, led to a near-unanimous approval by the Berkeley City Council for the ZNE design as proposed.

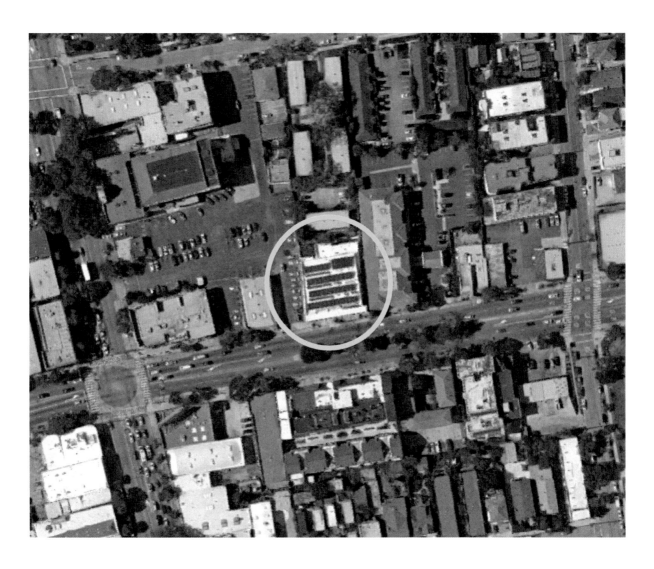

West Berkeley Branch Library: General Vicinity Plan

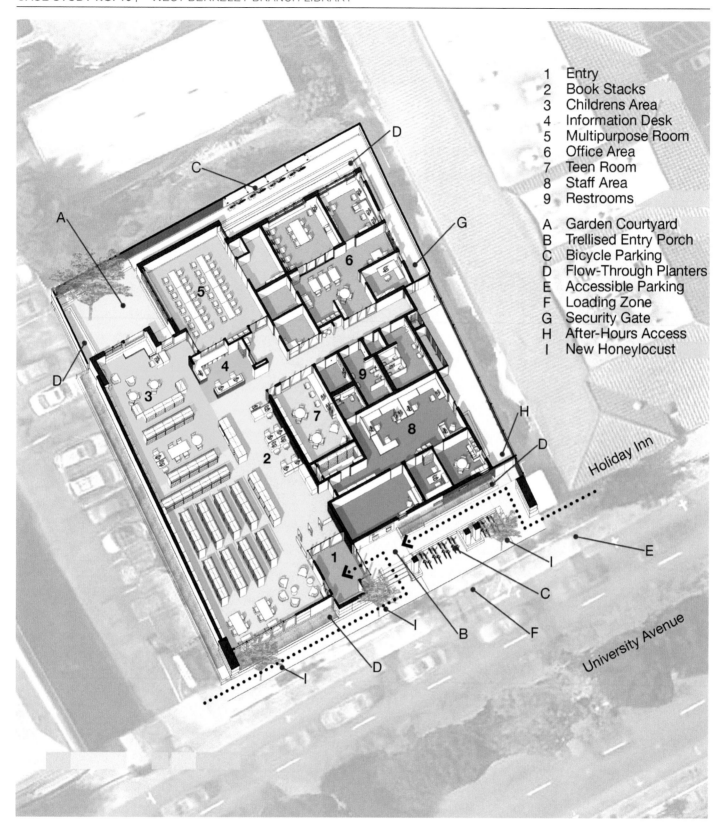

1 Entry
2 Book Stacks
3 Childrens Area
4 Information Desk
5 Multipurpose Room
6 Office Area
7 Teen Room
8 Staff Area
9 Restrooms

A Garden Courtyard
B Trellised Entry Porch
C Bicycle Parking
D Flow-Through Planters
E Accessible Parking
F Loading Zone
G Security Gate
H After-Hours Access
I New Honeylocust

West Berkeley Branch Library: Floor Plan

Design Process and Low Energy Design Strategies

The overall design process followed the traditional design and documentation phases, commencing with a concept design phase based on a previously completed master plan document that set both the construction budget and the building space program. Given the challenge of delivering a ZNE design, the project team continuously considered the energy aspect of every design idea and alternative as the process progressed from concept through detailed design.

Energy modeling was utilized to inform every decision, even at the concept design stage. Benchmark performance numbers, for example, were generated for basic scheme alternatives using "shoebox models" as representations of as-yet-to-be-determined final building forms. The impact of neighboring buildings on energy use and the relative availability of on-site renewable energy could be understood through similar simple studies at this early stage. These studies assisted in the overall evaluation of the alternative design schemes and the selection of the preferred scheme for later design study.

As the design advanced, more refined energy modeling, including daylight analysis and passive ventilation air flow analysis, was done to confirm or suggest modifications to the design. Combined with the routine cost estimates, the energy modeling provided a basis for decisions about energy-related materials and detailed constructions in order to keep the project on budget while still achieving ZNE performance. This continuing cost balancing exercise is generally central to a project such as this.

As proof of the accuracy of this process for the West Berkeley Branch Library, the final design was successfully bid under the prescribed project construction budget (less than 1% under), including all low-energy building features and the solar PV system. Based on the comparison with the originally prescribed first cost for the project for a code minimum building, the extra cost for the ZNE building design in this case was zero.

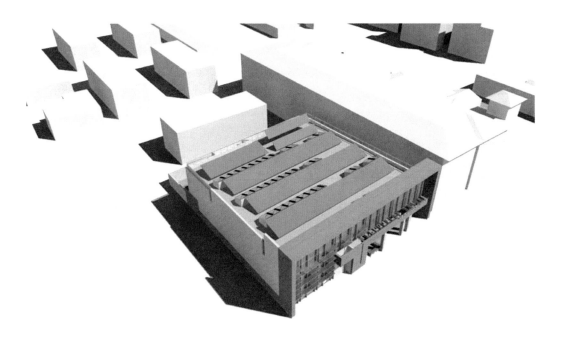

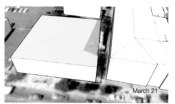

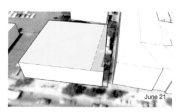

(Above) Shadow studies show that minimum roof height must be 24 feet to guarantee no shadowing from adjacent three-story building. (Diagram courtesy of Greenworks Studio).

(Below) "Shoebox" model including neighboring buildings—one existing and one potential future development.

Planning Concept and General Design Considerations

The concept design phase evaluated several alternative schemes for the small site, which was located in a commercial area along a very busy corridor connecting the Interstate highway with downtown Berkeley and the University of California campus. Design constraints on the schemes for this semi-urban site include the following:

- The city's zoning ordinance requires a minimum two-story facade for this area;
- The same ordinance states that direct sun at 12 noon on December 21 into adjacent property windows may not be blocked by the new building; because of the residential units to the north, this sets a constraining height for the building and its roof features, including any solar PV panel arrays;
- A three-story hotel is located five feet from the east property line, casting a shadow on the site in the early morning hours;
- Traffic noise level along this corridor was measured at 70 dBA within the footprint of the future building, preventing the possibility of openable windows for natural ventilation in the public library space.
- Two large California redwood trees in the northwest corner of the lot were to be protected, creating required open space on the small (12,000 sq. ft.) lot;
- The building program required a 9,500 sq. ft. building on the remaining buildable area of the site.

Several two-story schemes and a one-story scheme were evaluated programmatically and for best potential for a ZNE design. Solar and daylighting access was the key determinant of the selected scheme from among several alternatives considered. Studies showed quickly that the limited roof area and early morning shading from the adjacent hotel would set a likely maximum amount of on-site renewable energy available to the building over the course of year, and that this amount would be highest for a one-story scheme. The studies included capturing daylight for the spaces below the roof as well as solar energy for electric power generation.

Parallel studies of floor plan alternatives for library operations led to the same conclusion: a one-story scheme was most efficient, with a single service point rather than requiring a second one in the case of the two-story schemes.

"Shoebox" energy modeling of the alternative schemes indicated that a design EUI for the building of approximately 17-20 (kBtu/sq.ft. per year) would match the maximum on-site energy production possible with the one-story scheme. The two-story schemes, with the lower possible on-site energy production, would require a design EUI so low in order to achieve ZNE performance that it would not be feasible given the fixed construction budget amount.

(Right) University Avenue street elevation, showing urban context of the library building.

(Above) Building entrance area.

The scheme selected for design development was therefore the one-story scheme with a pre-scribed target of maximum EUI = 20 (kBtu/sq.ft. per year) and an expected on-site energy generation of 55,000 kWh from a 40 kW solar PV system[1]. The design would also be required to have western-style "false front" to satisfy the "two-story" frontage requirement of the city ordinance. The latter requirement also created the opportunity for a relatively high one-story public space within the building, which proved to be beneficial to the daylighting design for that space.

In general design terms, the design team chose a highly *passive* approach to reaching the EUI = 20 design target. In addition to focusing on daylighting as the principal opportunity for low-energy performance in this type of high-use lighting environment, the design team developed a passive method for moving air for ventilation, cooling and "night purging". (See discussion below.)

Energy modeling throughout the design phases verified that the target EUI was being achieved through each design iteration, indicating that the building was on track to perform at a ZNE level. As noted, the ZNE design features were also checked against cost impacts to confirm that the target budget was also being achieved.

Building Envelope

The height of the main public space and the desire to minimize thermal bridging through the structural studs of the exterior wall led to a choice of 3 X 8 wood *minilam*[2] studs for the wall framing, spaced at 24" apart. Cost criteria eliminated the idea of using a layer of rigid insulation on the exterior of the framing to eliminate any thermal bridging. Rock wool insulation fills the interstitial space between the studs, providing an advantage in both total assembly R-value (R=27.2) and control of any potential issues with indoor air quality because of its inorganic properties.

A simple truss-joist system was used for the roof, allowing a high level of insulation (R=49) and flexibility in locating the skylight arrays over the spaces below. The concrete floor slab is insulated below (R=10) since it is used for the radiant hydronic heating system. To avoid extra cost, the slab edge detail leaves a slight break in the continuity of the insulation layer from wall to floor.

---

[1] To determine the size in kW of a solar PV system based on the building's targeted or expected annual energy demand and the project site location, use the online tool provided by the U.S. National Renewable Energy Laboratory (NREL) at http://pvwatts.nrel.gov/.
[2] Laminated lumber product

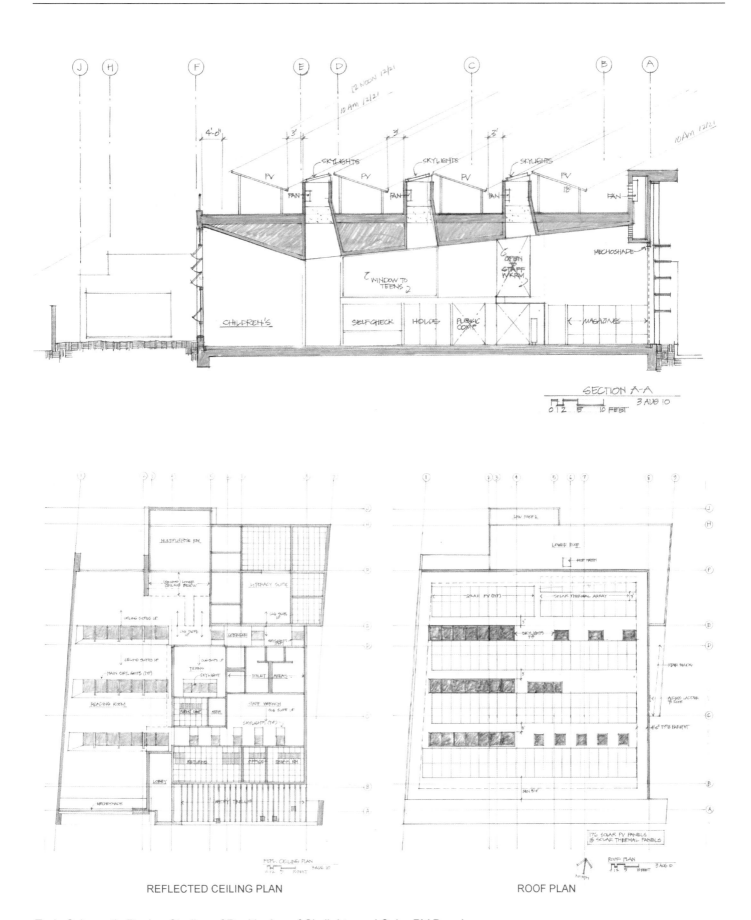

Early Schematic Design Studies of Positioning of Skylights and Solar PV Panels.

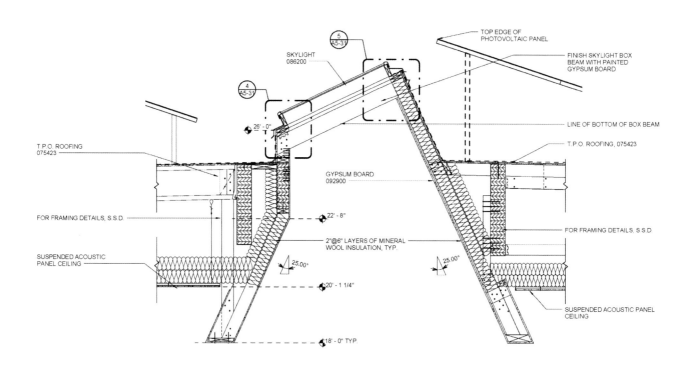

TOP EDGE OF PHOTOVOLTAIC PANEL

SKYLIGHT 086200

FINISH SKYLIGHT BOX BEAM WITH PAINTED GYPSUM BOARD

LINE OF BOTTOM OF BOX BEAM

T.P.O. ROOFING 075423

T.P.O. ROOFING, 075423

GYPSUM BOARD 092900

FOR FRAMING DETAILS, S.S.D.

FOR FRAMING DETAILS, S.S.D.

2"@6" LAYERS OF MINERAL WOOL INSULATION, TYP.

SUSPENDED ACOUSTIC PANEL CEILING

SUSPENDED ACOUSTIC PANEL CEILING

26' - 0"

22' - 8"

25.00°

25.00°

20' - 1 1/4"

18' - 0" TYP.

① Skylight above Stacks and Reading Room
SCALE: 3/4" = 1'-0"

children

PHOTO: DAVID WAKELY

Daylighting and Electric Lighting

Daylighting is intended as the principal design strategy for reducing overall energy use in the building, which is accomplished by offsetting the normally high electric load for lighting the book stacks and reading areas. To emphasize this intention, the ceiling plane in the main public space is designed as the principal architectural feature as well, with the diffusing surfaces below the skylight arrays forming a variety of daylighted surfaces canted at different angles to spread the diffuse daylight to the large space below.

The electric lighting design for the space is meant to reinforce this design concept as well. The thin LED strip lights mounted to the tops of the bookstacks are designed to provide all necessary task lighting when the daylight from the skylight arrays is not adequate. Similarly, LED reading lamps at tables provide the task lighting for the reading spaces. The appearance of the space in the evening would be quite different than during the day, to a degree unconventional in modern lighting design but perfectly adequate functionally. This design approach also avoids the visual distraction away from the daylighting design feature that would be caused by a conventional design of ceiling-mounted or large suspended electric light fixtures, drawing the eye to the plane of lighting below the skylights. A client-directed modification to this lighting design approach was made during the construction phase—see the discussion in *Post Occupancy: Lighting*, p. 28.

Internal spaces in the library (staff area, teen room) are designed with separate skylight groups that are positioned adjacent to internal walls so that these wall planes become diffuse sources of light to these spaces. Other smaller spaces, located at the perimeter, have high clerestory windows abutting the ceiling for the same lighting design effect.

The design process for daylighting followed steps similar to other case study projects: the roof-scape was carefully studied for the integration of the skylights and solar panel arrays since the roof area is limited and number of solar panels had to be maximized. The layout of these features was also constrained by the Berkeley Fire Department's requirement to leave a four-foot wide walking area around the edge of the roof itself. The daylighting design for the spaces below determined the basic location of the skylights and the solar panels were fit to the remaining allowable area.

PHOTO: KYLE JEFFERS

For cost reasons, the design team selected a standard square commercial skylight (4' X 4') and standard roof-mounting detail to create the skylight arrays. Rather than being set flat on the roof, the skylights are tilted at an angle of 25° toward the north. This tilt both avoids shading by the adjacent solar panel array and allows the skylight to "see" more of the brightest part of the luminous sky above[3,4].

Computer modeling[5] was used to adjust the design of the skylight arrays, in particular the geometry of the light-diffusing panels of the ceiling of the main room. Daylight level modeling indicated bands of lower footcandle levels at locations between the skylight arrays throughout the year. (See figure below.) As a result, the vertical shafts directly beneath the skylights were changed and the angles of the light-diffusing panels were spread wider to prevent daylight from being focused too much in the downward direction. Modeling of the adjusted design showed that the darker bands were eliminated and the daylight levels at 30 footcandles or above were more continuous across the space.

Modeling of the light levels in the public space confirmed that the standard lighting criteria for libraries[6] are satisfied over a large percentage of operating hours (>90%) for the horizontal reading surfaces and bookstack aisles, as well as the vertical light level at the lowest shelf in the bookstacks, without any overhead ceiling light fixtures.

(Right) Daylight Analysis, showing footcandle levels in main space BEFORE adjustment of daylight reflector panels below the skylights. (Bands of purple and dark blue colors signify less than 30 footcandles in that area between the arrays.)

Widening the apertures created by the reflector panels erases these bands and distributes the daylight uniformly across the space. No electric lighting is therefore needed to compensate for bands of low light levels.

(Diagrams courtesy of Greenworks Studio).

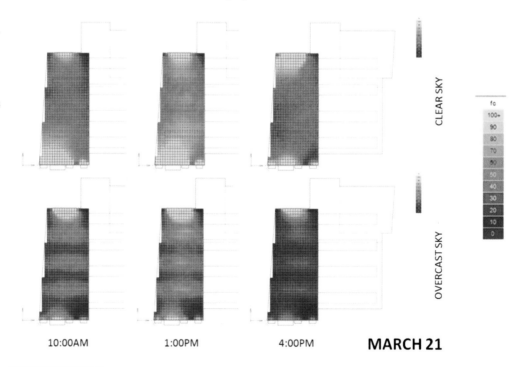

10:00AM   1:00PM   4:00PM   **MARCH 21**

---

[3] For this Bay Area location where marine conditions and cloudy skies are dominant, the sky is typically brighter at the zenith than at the horizon. The daylight collected is also proportional to the amount of sky "seen" by the daylight aperture, which is the *solid angle* subtended by the aperture.

[4] It is interesting to compare the daylight aperture designs of case studies #8, #9 and #10.

[5] The daylight models were first constructed in *Ecotect* then exported to *Daysim*, a *Radiance*-based daylight simulation tool provided by National Resource Canada. The results were then imported back into *Ecotect* for visualization.

[6] Illuminating Engineering Society, *Lighting Handbook 10th Edition*, https://www.ies.org/handbook/

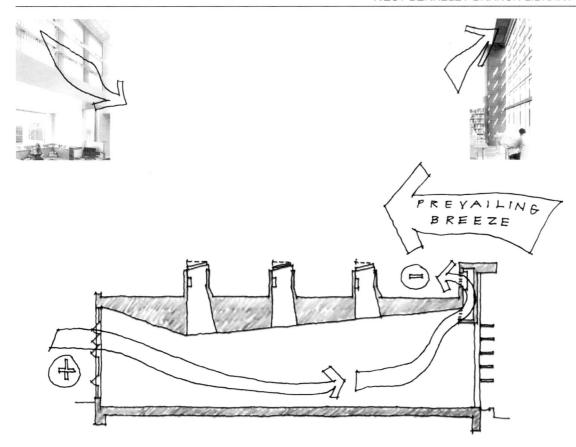

Natural Ventilation

The objective of the passive design approach for ventilation and cooling is to use wind pressure and the bouyancy of air to drive air movement through the building instead of using electricity for fans. Normally, *cross ventilation* via openable windows is an easy mechanism to design into buildings; when combined with good building control systems and a programmed sequence of operations, this can be done automatically and optimally for efficient heating and cooling. In this case study building, however, the high noise levels on the street side of the project site, combined with the code restrictions on openings in the zero-setback sides of the building, required a different approach.

The commercial district zoning ordinance required a two-story façade at the street, but this provided an opportunity to use a chimney effect to draw air through the building. The prevailing wind off of the nearby San Francisco Bay creates negative pressure at the back of the false-front structure of the façade, where several air ducts are embedded. These vertical ducts act essentially as *wind chimneys* that naturally draw air through the spaces from the north side due to the pressure difference, where automatically controlled operable windows act as the air inlets. (See diagram above.)

The amount of air moving through the spaces is determined by exterior temperature, interior CO_2 levels and the heating or cooling mode of operation in effect. Wind characteristics determine the need for the operation of low-power backup fans. (See the description of the *Mixed Mode of Operation* on the following page.) The building uses this natural ventilation system at all times, minimizing outdoor air flow to that required by code for fresh air during heating and cooling modes and maximizing the air flow when outdoor air temperatures can be used directly for cooling.

Particularly in mid-winter when the building is in heating mode, the injection of fresh air into the occupied space could create uncomfortable drafts. For this reason, the automatically controlled operable windows are equipped with hydronic convection heating grilles[7] on the interior. This proven system heats the incoming air to room temperature within inches of the window, thereby avoiding any cold draft effects. It is this feature that allows passive ventilation to be used year-round for fresh air.

---

[7] Runtal hydronic column radiators, http://www.runtalnorthamerica.com/residential_radiators/column-r-radiators.html.

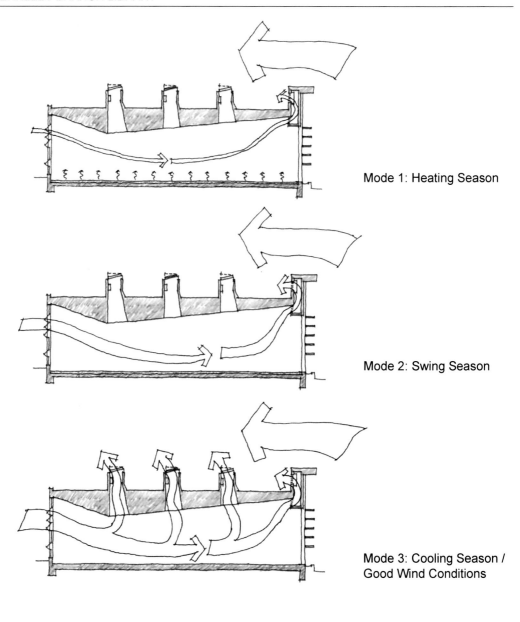

Mode 1: Heating Season

Mode 2: Swing Season

Mode 3: Cooling Season /
Good Wind Conditions

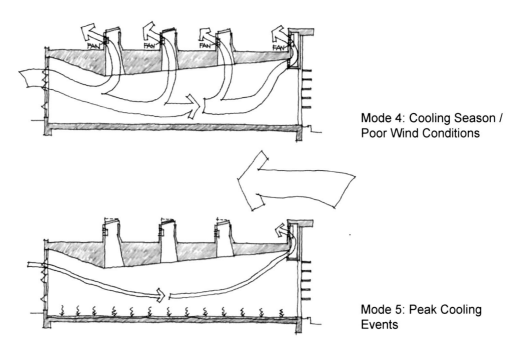

Mode 4: Cooling Season /
Poor Wind Conditions

Mode 5: Peak Cooling
Events

Diagrams by Edward Dean, FAIA

Proof of concept was provided by computer modeling of air flow through a three-dimensional model of the main space, using *computational fluid dynamics (CFD)* software[8] for different wind and temperature conditions. The computer modeling verified that even from high windows on the north side of the building, air would effectively and reliably move at the required volume flow rates through the space at the level of the occupants.

Heating, Ventilating and Cooling Systems

The basic mechanical heating and cooling system is a hydronic radiant system embedded in the concrete slab. The heating hot water is created by an array of solar thermal panels, with an auxiliary thermal storage tank. Three residential-size electric heat pumps provide backup to the solar thermal component so that sufficiently hot water is always available for the heating system. Currently, the solar thermal panels are providing about 50% of the total amount of energy for the hot water being used for radiant space heating. The air source heat pumps provide the balance.

The chilled water for cooling via the radiant slab is provided by the heat pump system. Because of the mild climate and small building size, the HVAC design is not a split-system where simultaneous mechanical heating and cooling in different zones may be required (as with Case Study No. 8, the IBEW-NECA Training Facility).

The building's total HVAC system is a combination of the radiant slab system and the passive ventilation system, controlled by the *building management system (BMS)* to function in a *Mixed Mode of Operation* so that energy use is minimized. The *sequence of operations* is programmed into the BMS so that all equipment and components function appropriately for each different mode of operation.

> Mode 1. Heating Season Operation. In this mode, the radiant heating system is on and the passive ventilation system admits the minimum amount of outdoor air as required by code.

> Mode 2. Swing Season Operation. No heating required and the amount of outdoor air required for fresh air and (at times) cooling varies. The wind chimney drives the air flow through the building spaces.

> Mode 3. Cooling Season Operation—Good Wind Conditions. Increased amounts of outside air are required for cooling purposes. Designated skylights open to allow movement of larger volumes of outdoor air.

> Mode 4. Cooling Season Operation—Poor Wind Conditions. System design includes back-up fans at skylight shafts to engage and ensure air flow under poor wind conditions and for *night purging*[9] using cool night air. (Skylights are closed.)

> Mode 5. Operation in Peak Cooling Events. Outdoor air is too warm for cooling, so full cooling mode with radiant slab cooling via heat pumps engages. The passive ventilation system admits the minimum amount of outdoor air as required by code.

The range of temperatures at which occupants are comfortable is increased by the use of large room fans in all but the large public space, where such fans would be impractical. These room fans are placed on manual control only, so occupants are required to understand their function and their availability. This was actually a problem for the general public in terms of best operation of these room fans—see the comments in *Post-Occupancy: HVAC*, p. 28.

---

[8] Airpak by Fluent Inc.
[9] *Night purging* involves flushing the building with cool night air in order to use the thermal mass of the building and its contents to pre-cool the building and absorb heat on the following day.

Domestic Hot Water

Hot water for use in the restrooms is provided via the solar thermal heating system using a heat transfer coil at the water storage tank.

Plug Loads

Much of the existing library equipment was to be used in the new building. In addition, the branch library planned to begin a program of providing laptop computers for patrons to use in the library for Internet access and general reading. A special literacy program, which was also going to be located in the new building, made heavy use of desktop computers that would be moved over. Initially at least, there was no funding option to replace this equipment with more energy efficient models. It was therefore essential to determine how large this plug load would be.

Measurements were made over several weeks to determine the average and peak power draw of all the equipment generating the plug load for the new building. This data was used in the whole building energy model to ensure reliable estimation of the building EUI and confirm that the building remained on track for ZNE performance.

Master System Integration and Control Systems

Unlike other case study buildings in this Volume, the design team for the West Berkeley Branch Library did not include a master system integrator to develop an omni-controller for all control systems related to the HVAC, lighting, solar PV, energy metering and energy dashboard during the design and documentation phases. Rather, separate control systems were specified and separately programmed by individual vendors, resulting in the similar problems and issues described in Volume 1 for earlier ZNE case study buildings. (*See Post-Occupancy Observations and Conclusions, below.*)

The controls subcontractor tasked with the programming of the HVAC *building management system (BMS)* was required to include coordination of the operation of all building components comprising the passive ventilation design—the automatic windows and skylights in relation to the *Mixed Mode of Operation* for the entire HVAC system, the weather measurement system and the CO_2 sensors. With construction partially completed, the subcontractor also took on the task of incorporating the controls for the solar PV system, the energy metering system and the setup of the energy dashboard. This required a change order and extra cost to the project since this work had not been defined and planned beforehand. The development of an "omni-control" system essentially evolved during the construction phase, carried out by the BMS controls vendor.

The final "omni-control" system, however, is not quite complete since the control systems related to daylighting and electric lighting, including daylight sensors and dimming controls, were executed separately by the electrical subcontractor.

The controls subcontractor did not continue in any kind of maintenance or advisory role after the completion of construction. Tracking of the building energy performance since that date has been done by the director of the Office of Energy and Sustainable Development for the City of Berkeley on an intermittent basis. Building systems operation has been the responsibility of the maintenance staff of the Berkeley Public Library.

Commissioning

Commissioning was carried out by a third-party commissioning agent and included all the commissioning requirements for LEED certification. However, once the commissioning activities in the construction phase were completed, no further commissioning was done by this agent. (*See Post-Occupancy Observations and Conclusions, below.*)

Renewable On-Site Energy Supply

The renewable energy system as installed consists of 120 solar photovoltaic panels rated at 435 watts (DC) per panel, for a system size of 52.2 kW, with an estimated annual energy supply of 75,000 kWh. The final bid specification called for 160 panels rated at 315 watts per panel, for a system size of 50.4 kW. This was still an over-sizing of the system compared to the modeled building demand of 55,000 kWh, which would require only a 40 kW system. The oversizing by about 30% correlates directly with the measured overproduction of the system. (See *Energy Production versus Energy Use: Zero Net Energy*, below.) A certain amount of oversizing was deliberate, as noted in the *ZNE Design Development Report* to the client:

> It is expected that higher performing panels will be available for comparable price at the time of bidding in late 2011, so that an excess capacity is likely. The excess capacity is desired since actual energy use may be higher than modeled. The models assume a cautious but nevertheless ideal schedule of operation and use, as well as many assumptions about plug load, the largest component of electrical load expected.

There are also sixteen solar thermal panels mounted on the north edge of the roof to avoid casting a large shadow on the PV panels or skylights. The solar thermal panels provide the base hot water used in the radiant slab heating system. Originally specified to be tilted at an angle of 45°, the installed solar thermal panel array has a 15° tilt, matching that of the solar PV panels. This field adjustment essentially requires the heat pump backup system to operate more often, but was done to avoid casting long shadows into windows of neighboring apartments.

Energy Design Analysis and Energy Performance:
Modeling versus Post-Occupancy Measurements

Energy Use — Modeling

Energy modeling was carried out during the design phases using an early version of *Design-Builder* (v.2.1). The principal uses for the modeling results were to benchmark the energy demand and to confirm that a ZNE performance for the building would be feasible with the maximum size solar PV system that could be installed on the roof. As design decisions were made, often based on cost criteria, the energy model was used to confirm that the energy demand did not drift upward.

DesignBuilder utilizes *EnergyPlus* as the simulation engine and, as a result, does not model well the passive ventilation in this particular building design. Some manual estimates were made for the energy savings from the use of the passive ventilation for daytime cooling and night purging, then applied to the modeling results. The model was subsequently updated using DesignBuilder v4.5.0.178.

The final design model yielded a total annual energy use of 47,700 kWh, or an EUI of 17.5 kBtu/sq. ft. per year.

Energy Use — Actual Measurement and Comparison to Modeling Results

The original bid documents required that each electrical panel be equipped with branch circuit power meters for monitoring individual circuit loads. This specification was later changed to one power meter per panel, with each of three panels designated to all lighting, all plug load circuits and all mechanical equipment. The data from these three power meters was recorded over the course of a year (2014); the accompanying charts summarize the annual and monthly energy demand for each of these three principal types of electric loads.

PHOTO: EDWARD DEAN

Modeled Energy Use
(Annual)

47,500 kWh/year
Modeled EUI =17.5

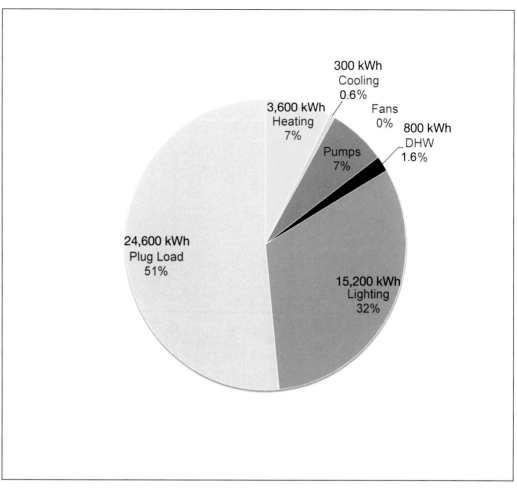

Measured Energy Use
(2014)

63,000 kWh/year
Measured EUI = 23.1

"Mechanical" =
Heating, Cooling, Pumps,
Fans and DHW

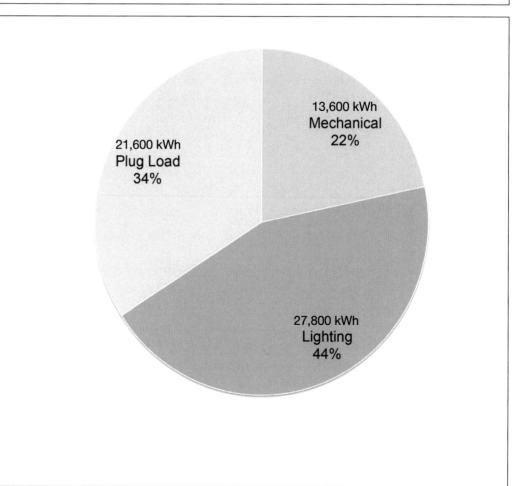

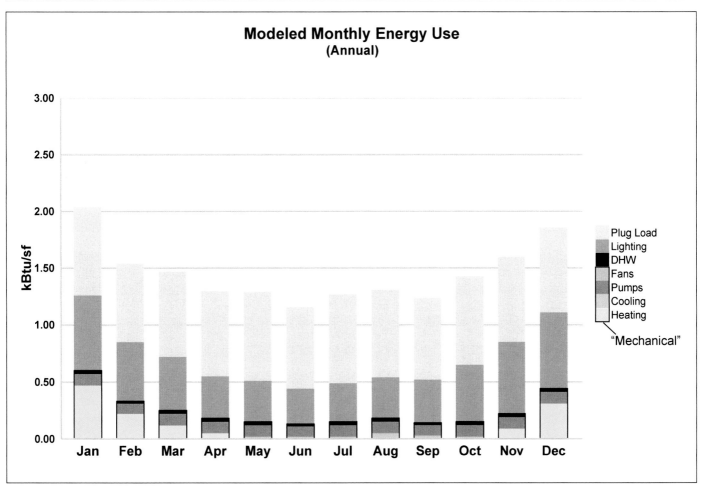

Modeled Monthly Energy Use
(Annual)

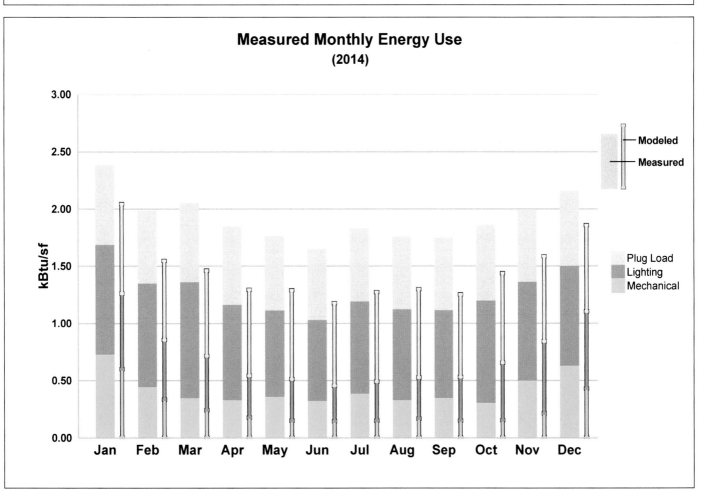

Measured Monthly Energy Use
(2014)

The metering setup did not permit separate data reporting for heating, cooling, ventilation and pump energy use. Hence the energy use categories indicated for the energy modeling results cannot be separately reported for the measured results, and therefore compared. The charts showing measured data combine these four categories into the single category of "Mechanical".

The total energy used by the building in this year was 63,000 kWh, or an EUI = 23.1 kBtu/sf per year. This total is approximately 15% more than the design target and 30% more than that indicated by the energy modeling. The whole building energy model was not calibrated to actual weather and occupancy conditions, but some reasons for the difference are the incomplete commissioning after the building was occupied, as well as some user behavior issues that arose. (See *Post Occupancy: Observations and Conclusions*, below.)

Energy Production versus Energy Use: Zero Net Energy

While the energy use was higher in this first year of occupancy than the design target, the over-sized solar PV system provided the cushion needed to exceed the goal of ZNE performance. The system performed as specified in the submittal by the solar subcontractor, providing 75,000 kWh during the year, about 20% more than the energy used in that period.

The *Cumulative Energy Balance* chart for 2014 illustrates the net positive performance of the building, with the net total on-site energy balance at the end of that one-year period still positive on the production side.

Post Occupancy: Observations and Conclusions

Perhaps the most successful aspect of this case study project is the fact that the new building incorporates systems and features that result in a ZNE performance within the fixed first-cost budget established for the project. The project cost budget, established by a professional consulting team years earlier and never envisioning any more than a basic LEED-Silver building design, was absolutely fixed by the public bond measure—no additional funds would be available. Yet, the design team and the client worked successfully together to expand the project goal to a *zero-net-energy* building and to achieve that goal within the cost budget, at the same time with all other project requirements fulfilled.

The project experienced problems and issues on the path to this success, however, not unlike the other successful case study buildings. There are still common technical issues, but for public projects there are some differences created by the public process and occupant behavior that can affect the final design and the actual performance.

Post Occupancy: Controls and Monitoring

The need for a master controls integrator became obvious at the start of commissioning when the relative complexity of the sequence of operations of the passive ventilation system became apparent, along with the other aspects of the mechanical systems operation. Large parts of this system are not normally centrally controlled by a conventional *building management system (BMS)*, yet the BMS controls technician was required to program the system to operate windows, skylights, shades, backup ventilation fans, as well as to respond to inputs from the rooftop weather station and the interior CO_2 sensors.

As noted in the controls system description above, the BMS vendor was given a change order to add the solar PV system, the small metering system and the energy dashboard to the central control system. Except for the metering system, which uses a Modbus communication protocol, these added operating control systems use BACnet protocol.

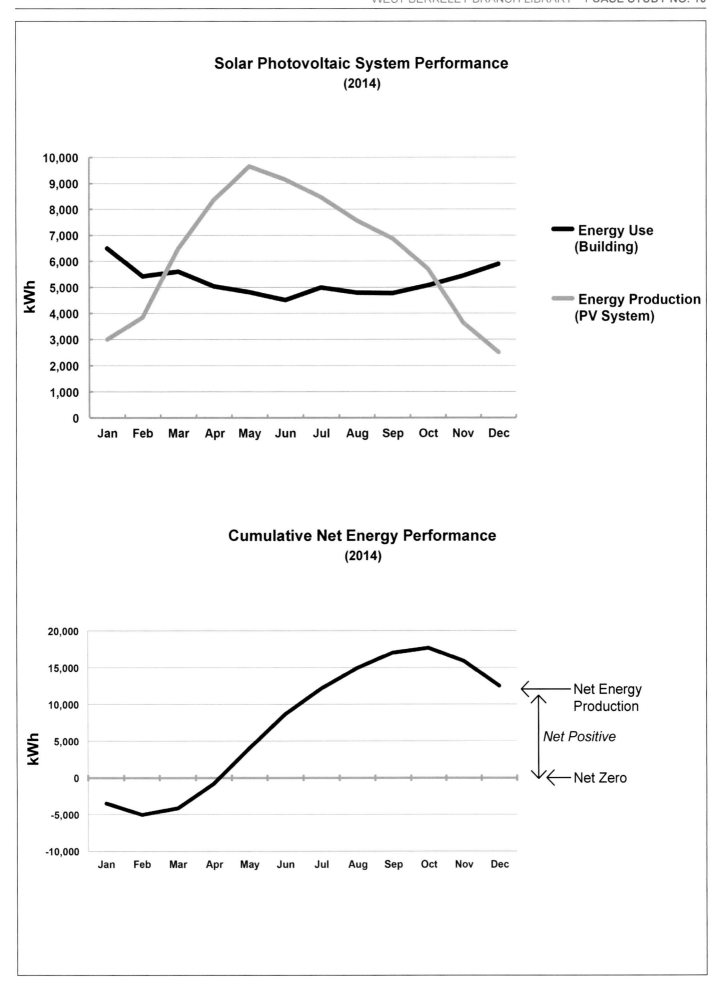

Programming the BMS for the multi-mode operation with the passive ventilation approach proved to be challenging for the controls technician given the different thermal zones even in a building this small. Different modes of operation in some zones are often required on mild days—heating in one zone while opening windows for passive ventilation cooling in another zone, for example.

Upon completion of this system programming, the controls technician left the project and no maintenance contract for the controls system was put in place for the early occupancy period, something that is highly recommended to ensure proper controls system operation in the first years of building operation.

There was also a particular problem with the controls for the window actuators, which automatically open the windows as required for fresh air or for larger quantities of cooling air. Like most window actuators currently available in the U.S., those specified for this building have only two settings: they are in a "fully open" position or a "fully closed" position. That is, no partially open position is normally possible. However, when only the minimum amount of fresh air is needed in a particular zone during the heating mode, for example, the ventilating window should open only a minimal amount.

This proved to be a major flaw in the design since cold drafts were created in the winter when the CO_2 sensor called for the minimum fresh air and the window moved to the fully open position. The solution by the maintenance staff to the draft problem was to set a higher threshold at the CO_2 sensor so that the windows remained shut, creating some feeling of discomfort within the space. (Note that the same problem was encountered in Case Study #9, the *435 Indio Way Office Building*, but the master system integrator for that building solved the problem by programming the control for the actuators to stop at intermediate open positions. Since the controls integrator for West Berkeley Branch Library was not engaged for the post-occupancy period, this option was not considered.)

Lack of experience with this type of system combined with the late development of the master control system led to this type of issue. Another example is the design of the controls sequence in case of rainy weather. In this case, all passive ventilation for cooling is terminated—windows and skylights close and cannot be opened, even for the fresh air requirement. The system simply switches to radiant cooling using the heat pump. Better coordination of rain protection options at the operable windows and a smarter controls sequence would avoid this default to mechanical cooling in case of rain.

In general, the building operation problems related to building control systems that were encountered with this building in the first year of occupancy highlight the need to engage the master control system integrator beginning in the design phase and, via some kind of maintenance contract, through at least the first year of occupancy. The continuity is important, as is the obvious coordination with the building commissioning agent.

Post Occupancy: HVAC

The post-occupancy experience with the HVAC systems primarily involved the BMS and commissioning the proper sequence for the different modes of operation for heating, cooling and ventilation, as described in the previous section. There were, however, a number of smaller issues that arose that are instructive to consider from the perspective of user interaction with the design intent.

The passive ventilation system is designed to operate independently of the occupants in order to ensure proper operation of the entire system in an efficient manner, much like not allowing inexperienced passengers to intervene with a self-operating sailboat. Thus, the operable windows are located high on the wall, out of reach of building occupants, automatically operated by the BMS.

The design team, understanding the value of providing occupants with some local control in a naturally ventilated building with a broad range of temperature swings, provided for a single manually operable window in most spaces to enhance the sense of control and comfort. In the meeting room, however, the automatically-controlled windows are, because of the low ceiling, within reach of the occupants.

Because of the actuator issue described in the previous section, on the first occasion when the meeting room became stuffy and uncomfortable, one of the automatically operating windows was forced open and broken. This is perceived as a design issue that can be addressed with an alternative approach in this type of room, such as utilizing operating in-wall air dampers rather than controlled windows.

Another issue pertains to the design of the *hydronic convection heating grilles* located just inside the automatically operable windows. The grilles are manufactured with metal flat bars at a specific geometry and spacing to ensure that cold outside air is heated to room temperature over the short distance as the air passes over these flat bars. After the grilles were installed, some library staff complained that the appearance of the flat bar grilles suggested incarceration. The client ordered a change in the geometry—a wider spacing of the convective flat bars that make up the grille, to mitigate this visual association. The effect was also to reduce the heat transfer and warming of incoming air, resulting in complaints of cold drafts near the operable windows.

Finally, the large room fans were placed under manual control only, which resulted in infrequent operation even when the cooling effect would be substantial, or excessively high speeds because of lack of understanding of the purpose of this feature. In public spaces where users are likely to lack information about the operational design of a ZNE building, it is probably better to have the large room fans operate automatically as part of the passive cooling modes, with a manual "off" switch at each fan for local user control.

Post Occupancy: Commissioning

Standard commissioning was carried out for this case study project and was completed approximately at the start of occupancy in January 2014. Similarly, the related programming and development of the master control system for all but the lighting systems was wrapped up at the same time. Neither the commissioning agent nor the controls contractor continued with the project after the start of building occupancy. The building operations and maintenance was turned over to the maintenance supervisor for Berkeley Public Library with little transition instruction or training.

Issues with operations, metering and unusual energy use continued for some time after occupancy, as would be expected in this situation. Activities during this initial period should be regarded as ongoing commissioning and are best accomplished with continuity from construction through initial occupancy. The two principal objectives during post-occupancy are:

- Continuous "re-commissioning" of the equipment and system functionality for energy efficiency;

- Calibration (and re-calibration) of power meters, flow meters, sensors and gauges. These devices tend to drift from their initial set points soon after the first commissioning is done.

Post Occupancy: Lighting

The daylighting design for the main public space features the large skylight arrays that provide adequate lighting for 90% of the open hours. For remaining hours and dark days, the LED stack lighting provides the balance of light required to meet library lighting level standards for horizontal and vertical (face of book titles in the stacks) illumination, as noted in the discussion of the approach to the lighting design. During construction and before wall finishes were applied, how-ever, the client expressed concern about the light levels (despite the results of the daylight mod-eling and overall lighting level simulations) as well as the visibility of the space from the street through the large south-facing window. The concern was that the library might be misunderstood to be *closed* if the space were illuminated by daylight only. Other commercial enterprises along this busy street would have their electric lights turned on, indicating "open for business", but the library would not.

The design team was directed to add suspended overhead electric light fixtures to the space even though the fixtures were not necessary for illumination purposes. Large, circular suspended LED fixtures were added to the space in response to this directive. The large space now basically has two electric lighting systems, each of which can separately provide the electric lighting necessary for backup of the daylighting skylight system—the distributed bookstack-mounted lights and the ceiling-suspended light fixtures. In addition, the visual effect is to reduce the perceived height of the space to the plane of the suspended light fixtures and obscure the appearance of the shaped ceiling designed to optimize the daylighting effect.

This issue was compounded by the fact that no dimming controls are currently operational. For the purposes of having the suspended light fixtures be indicators of "open for business", the manual controls for these fixtures were locked in the *on* position. The measured energy use data indicates this high level of electric light energy being used.

There has been some effort to modify this operation and to revert to the original design intent of having all electric lighting under dimmable controls responding to the daylight sensors. However, the backup electric lighting systems, the distributed bookstack-mounted lights and the ceiling-suspended overhead lights, remain essentially redundant.

Post Occupancy: Occupant Behavior

Some of the interventions by building occupants are described above. The general design con-cept to separate the operation of passive systems from occupant control and make it automatic is best when these systems are integrated with the overall operation of the building systems. It is important for optimal results, however, to design as well the allowable options for user control of certain aspects of these systems. Not only is interference avoided, but the informed occupant can also make better use of these options to customize comfort conditions and often improve energy efficiency.

At the *West Berkeley Branch Library*, the library staff in particular did not initially understand the operational design of the building; they modified settings or used override switches as they would in a conventional building. A special meeting was arranged so that details of operation could be explained and how their user behaviors would result in lower energy use and a smaller carbon footprint for the building. The observed result of this effort to fully inform the staff seems to be a supportive attitude toward the target of accomplishing a ZNE performance for the building by the end of the year, which was indeed achieved, as well as smarter use of the building in general.

All of the case studies point to the advantages of a fully-informed and fully-supportive user group. For private clients and owners, this is an easier goal. Special efforts to provide information and training for public user groups seem to be required and should be planned as part of the transi-tion to the new space.

The Exploratorium

PHOTO: BRUCE DAMONTE

The Exploratorium
Case Study No. 11

Data Summary

Building Type: Museum (Inter-active)

Location: San Francisco, CA

Gross Floor Area (Pier 15): 192,914 gsf (excluding 7,605 sf of restaurant/cafe tenant space)

Occupied: 2013

Energy Modeling Software: eQuest v. 3.64

Modeled EUI (Site): 45.6 kBtu/sf-year

Measured EUI (Site): 42.0 kBtu/sf-year (2015)

On-Site Renewable Energy System Installed: 1,400 kW (DC) Solar PV

Measured On-Site Energy Production:
2,000 MWh/year (2014)
1,991 MWh/year (2015)
36.0 kBtu/sf-year (2015)

Measured Solar Thermal Production: Separate data not available

Owner/Client

The Exploratorium

Design Team

Architect: EHDD Architecture, San Francisco, CA

Structural Engineer: Rutherford & Chekene, San Francisco, CA

Mechanical/Plumbing Engineer: Integral Group, Oakland, CA

Electrical Engineer: Cammisa & Wipf, San Francisco, CA

Lighting Design: David Nelson & Associates, Littleton, CO

Landscape Architect: GLS Landscape Architecture, San Francisco, CA

General Contractor

Nibbi Brothers

All but one of the case study buildings described in this volume are major renovations of general building shells to accommodate new uses while achieving a performance goal of annual zero net energy use. Case Study No. 11. *The Exploratorium*, is by far the largest and most extensive of these, transforming an empty waterfront warehouse structure built on a pier into a modern science museum. While this building is, from one point of view, a special case because of its unique site, unique program and unique design constraints, it is nevertheless a good example of the common issues that arise with ZNE design of buildings of all types and the design process involved in resolving them.

As in the case of the other ZNE case study buildings, some standard ZNE design strategies were not possible due to the strong design constraints imposed on many aspects of the project. As with the other ZNE projects, the design team developed compensating and augmenting strategies to approach successfully the ZNE performance goal in the context of the overall design solution.

Background

The Exploratorium is classified as a *science museum*, but the building program and user experience do not fit the standard characterizations of this type of facility. Rather than housing standard passive exhibits of scientific facts and devices, the facility is experiential, exploratory and interactive, with the intention that the building visitor discover scientific ideas and concepts in an encouraged active manner.

The focus of the public spaces is self-teaching and exploration of natural phenomena through hands-on activities. The participation of artists in the design of these spaces enhances the idea of exploration of the intersection of art and science and creates an ambience of inquiry and discovery.

This approach to public education in the sciences and the history of the development of the vision for this institution directly affect the nature of the new space, the many architectural decisions and ultimately the design strategies adopted to achieve the goal of zero net energy performance. This process was made even more complex by the building location selected for the Exploratorium's new home. To understand the effect of the many design constraints and the selected ZNE design strategies, it is useful to have some background details about the institution, its history and the special nature of the new location.

The original idea for the Exploratorium as an approach to teaching scientific principles to the public was developed by Frank Oppenheimer, an experimental physicist and university professor. Convinced that education in scientific methodologies could occur through "museum" facilities that supplemented regular educational curricula at all levels and that incorporated a well-designed discovery approach, Oppenheimer embarked in 1965 on a study of science museums around the world. By 1969, he had successfully developed the details of the idea and secured financial support from organizations and individuals in the San Francisco community. That year, he opened the original Exploratorium facility in that city in *The Palace of Fine Arts (PFA)*, a building left over from the 1915 Pan Pacific Exposition. The culture of hands-on inquiry, which was the focus from the first day it opened, has remained at the heart of the institution's mission since that time.

After 25 years or so, the Exploratorium started to experience the limits of the PFA space and began to discuss options for new space. Ready public access and the availability of space into which the Exploratorium could continue to grow in the future were prime considerations. Finally, after years of discussion, fundraising and searches, the Port of San Francisco proposed that the Exploratorium take over the warehouse structures on Piers 15 and 17 of the main waterfront,

The Exploratorium: General Vicinity Plan

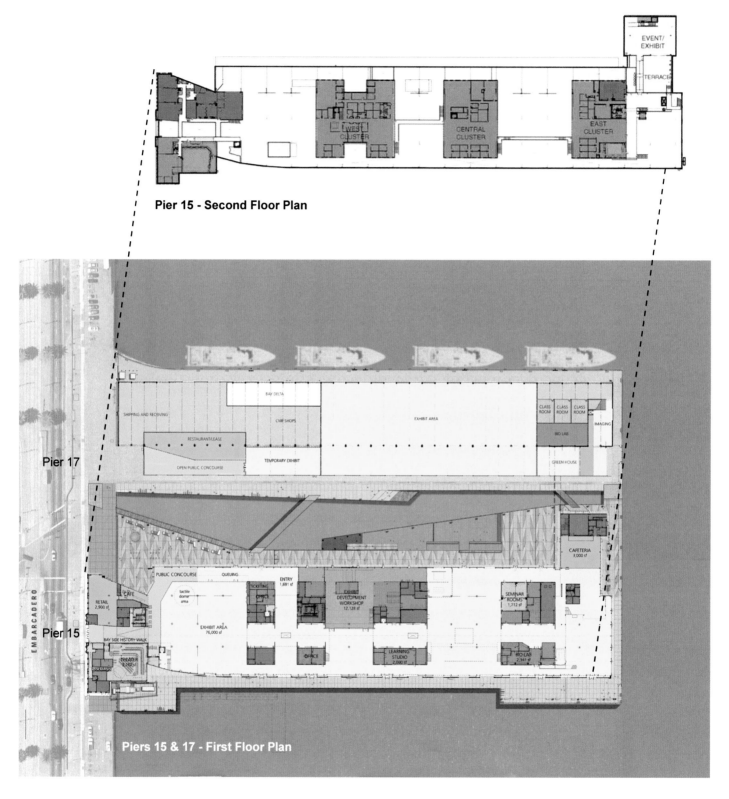

Pier 15 - Second Floor Plan

WEST CLUSTER

CENTRAL CLUSTER

EAST CLUSTER

EVENT/ EXHIBIT

TERRACE

Pier 17

Pier 15

SHIPPING AND RECEIVING

BAY DELTA

CMP SHOPS

EXHIBIT AREA

CLASS ROOM

CLASS ROOM

CLASS ROOM

IMAGING

BIO LAB

RESTAURANT/LEASE

TEMPORARY EXHIBIT

GREEN HOUSE

OPEN PUBLIC CONCOURSE

CAFETERIA 3,000 sf

PUBLIC CONCOURSE

QUEUING

ENTRY 1,691 sf

TICKETING

OFFICE

EXHIBIT DEVELOPMENT WORKSHOP 12,128 sf

SEMINAR ROOMS 1,712 sf

RETAIL 2,900 sf

CAFE

tactile dome area

EXHIBIT AREA 76,000 sf

OFFICE

LEARNING STUDIO 2,000 sf

BIO LAB 2,341 sf

BAY SIDE HISTORY WALK

THEATER 2,262 sf

EMBARCADERO

Piers 15 & 17 - First Floor Plan

The Exploratorium: Floor Plans

the Embarcadero, which had been seriously damaged in the 1989 Loma Prieta earthquake and were at risk of being torn down.

At this point, the Embarcadero had been designated a *National Historic District* and the two piers were listed on the National Register of Historic Places, administered by the U. S. National Park Service. The Exploratorium's Board of Directors recognized the value of prime public exposure and access at the Embarcadero as well as the large amoiunt of available space for current and future development (roughly 200,000 sq. ft. at Pier 15 and an equal amount of interior space at Pier 17). The Board began negotiating for the lease in 2006 and the Port Commission authorized an exclusive agreement. Finally, with the support of San Francisco's Board of Supervisors, the Exploratorium signed a 66-year lease in 2009 for the two piers and their warehouse buildings.

Once the basic decision was made about the future location for the Exploratorium, the roadmap could be laid out for the completion of the project with all its goals achieved, including the advanced goal of constructing a large museum facility capable of ZNE performance. The roadmap also pointed to the many challenges and design constraints along the path to this goal, as described in the following paragraphs.

Historic Preservation Restrictions

With the designation, "registered national historic structures", the two piers came under the strict administrative control of the both the National Park Service (NPS) and the California State Historic Preservation Office (SHPO). All design renovation decisions were required to pass the scrutiny of these two agencies and obtain their final approval for anything affecting the historic "character" of the structures. This would affect almost every aspect of the ZNE design strategies and final decisions.

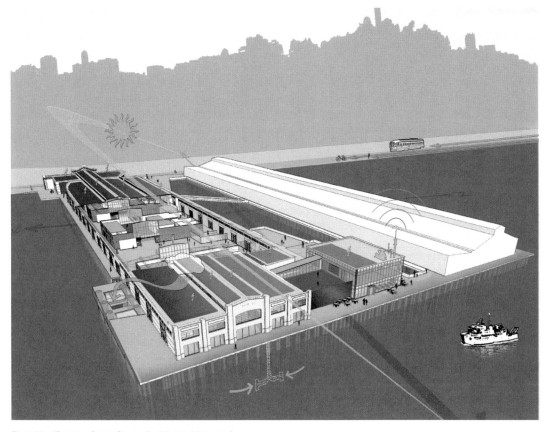

Bay-side view of Exploratorium piers BEFORE renovaton

PHOTO: EHDD ARCHITECTURE

Multitude of Governing Agencies and Stakeholder Groups

In addition to NPS and SHPO, which controlled every aspect of the project related to the historic character of the site and buildings, there were 12 other regulatory agencies and 17 stakeholder groups that had authority for review and approval of design decisions pertaining to many different aspects of the building and site design. This inevitably affected the nature of some ZNE design features.

For example, the *Bay Conservation and Development Commission (BCDC)* placed many requirements and restrictions on the use of San Francisco Bay water that was planned for a water-source heat pump system. Similarly, the *Telegraph Hill Neighborhood Association* insisted that the solar photovoltaic panels be installed flat to the existing roof to minimize visual impact to the neighborhood, which is located a half-mile away.

Building Program and Hands-On Exhibits

The popular building program guarantees large crowds of visitors daily, totaling over 500,000 people per year. The many hands-on exhibits in the space ordinarily require a high concentration of specific types of lighting as well as equipment that creates an unusual type of *plug load* for the building. While energy demand is considered in the exhibit design, the principal requirement is the functionality and design of the exhibit itself. Higher than normal lighting and plug loads were therefore expected.

Existing Structures

The piers and warehouse structures had suffered extensive damage in the 1989 earthquake and, in any event, would require structural upgrades for modern seismic safety requirements for a public facility such as this. Combined with the historic restrictions on the visibility of these upgrades, energy-related design features had to be incorporated in unique ways. (See the discussion in *Building Envelope* below.)

Environmental Constraints

A logical approach to the design of an energy-efficient HVAC system was to take advantage of the presence of unlimited quantities of bay water beneath the piers. The salty water is corrosive, however, and is filled with organic materials including small animals. Tight regulatory control exists over the water quality, temperature and wildlife protection measures. In addition, maintenance and operations issues had to be addressed in the design of all aspects of the bay-related building systems. (See the discussion in *Heating, Ventilating and Cooling Systems* below.)

Design Process and Low Energy Design Strategies

The design team had participated in early studies of the relocation of the Exploratorium facilities, including an evaluation of the pier site when the opportunity arose to obtain a long-term lease for that highly desirable location. When the property was committed to the Exploratorium in 2006, the Board of Directors held a visioning session with its staff and the design team to develop goals and strategies. At this visioning session the design team proposed the idea of designing toward a ZNE-performing facility. The Board and the rest of the participants embraced this proposal as consistent with the institution's mission, which includes demonstrating to the public technical concepts about their local environment.

Having adopted the goal for ZNE performance, the design team set about developing a set of ZNE design strategies that could be utilized within the many constraints outlined above. It was clear from the beginning that the most serious limitations would be on the building envelope efficiencies and the likely plug loads and electric lighting energy demand, but that very high efficiencies in the design of the heating and cooling systems might be achieved with the ready availability of the bay water.

Bay-side view of Exploratorium piers AFTER renovaton

PHOTO: BRUCE DAMONTE

Planning Concept and General Design Considerations

The general design approach was to capture and channel the familiar informality of the original Exploratorium space at the PFA and, in recognition of the new historic location, to emphasize the existing character and original sense of place of the San Francisco waterfront. The ZNE design, like the architectural expression in general, harmonizes with this concept at every level of detail and is a functional backdrop to the program in the public spaces.

When the Exploratorium took over the two piers, the property consisted of the two warehouse structures, a heavily damaged pier support structure consisting of original timber pilings and a large covered parking lot that was built between the two piers. (See accompanying photo of the original pier components.) Because the parking lot had been added much later, its removal was deemed consistent with the historic renovation process.

Since Pier 17 is relegated to support space and future expansion, its structures received only basic code renovation for these purposes and is not included in the public program spaces. This ZNE Case Study No. 11 therefore consists only of the building complex on Pier 15, the renovated steel and concrete warehouse structure that was originally built in 1931 and the new building wing that is added at the end of that pier. Pier 17 is not considered part of the ZNE building.

The building design program consists of the public hands-on galleries, a small theater, a webcast studio, classrooms, training rooms and administrative offices. A separate space customized for large events, a San Francisco Bay Observatory and a commercial restaurant are accommodated in the new building wing placed at the end of Pier 15. The restaurant is a tenant space that is also not included as part of The Exploratorium's ZNE boundary[1].

Substantial structural improvements had to be done to both the piers and the warehouse buildings. Since they would be invisible from above, new six-foot diameter piles could be installed as part of the structural strengthening of the pier decks. In addition, for Pier 15, the structural diaphragms of both the warehouse deck floor and the roof had to be stiffened substantially, requiring a solution that retained the historic character while contributing to the ZNE performance in a largely invisible way.

---

[1] The one exception is that the energy used by the radiant floor heating system in the tenant space is included in the annual energy use of the ZNE building and this energy is currently supplied to the tenant without charge.

PHOTO: BRUCE DAMONTE

Embarcadero-side view of Exploratorium Pier 15 after renovaton *(Left)*

Building Envelope

Historic preservation factors were the principal determinant for much of the building envelope. This strongly affected the design choices for optimal energy performance and achieving ZNE.

The walls are built of steel structural frames and 8" thick concrete panels—very thermally conductive materials and constructions with much thermal bridging. The exterior and interior appearance of these walls was deemed to be *contributory* to the historic character of the building, which required that no changes be made—specifically that no insulation layer with new finish could be applied. Single glazing could be replaced with high-performance double-glazed units, however, since the appearance was not noticeably different if the window frames were suitably replicated. (The exception to this was the glass installed at several locations where industrial wire-glass was first used in 1931, an innovation at the time. These glass areas were required to remain as single-glazed wire glass units.)

The surface area of the walls is much less than that of the floor and roof, however, so thermal losses are actually dominated by the latter building surfaces. The interior surface of the roof structure and roof sheathing could not be disturbed because of its historic nature, so a second roof was created on the outside surface and a cavity between the two roofs was filled with insulation, bringing the roof R-value to a substantial R-28.

This solution at the roof greatly assisted with the building's ZNE performance goal, but it also resulted in the need to raise the sills of the roof monitors because of the added thickness of the overall roof system. Fortunately, the governing historic agencies determined that the visual impact of this change was small enough to allow the installation of the insulating layer and replacement of the roof monitor windows with high performance assemblies.

The structural strengthening of the floor system and pier deck had more significant impacts on the historic structure. To provide a sufficiently strong structural floor diaphragm, a new concrete floor system of beams-and-slab, resembling a structural "waffle" slab system, was proposed to be installed on top of the existing concrete pier deck. This design provides an opportunity for an integrated solution for the historic preservation, structural and ZNE performance objectives:

- The structural requirement for a sufficiently strong floor diaphragm is satisfied with a minimal impact to the existing historic structure;

PHOTO: BRUCE DAMONTE

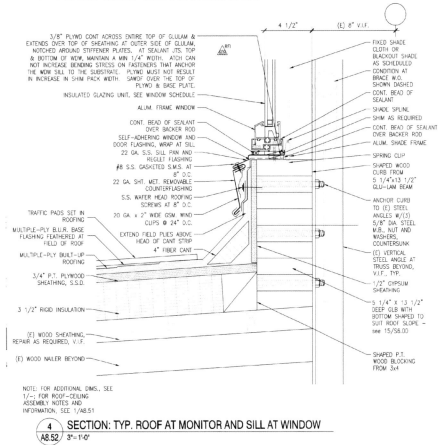

3/8" PLYWD CONT ACROSS ENTIRE TOP OF GLULAM &
EXTENDS OVER TOP OF SHEATHING AT OUTER SIDE OF GLULAM,
NOTCHED AROUND STIFFENER PLATES. AT SEALANT JTS. TOP
& BOTTOM OF WDW, MAINTAIN A MIN 1/4" WIDTH. ATCH CAN
NOT INCREASE BENDING STRESS ON FASTENERS THAT ANCHOR
THE WDW SILL TO THE SUBSTRATE. PLYWD MUST NOT RESULT
IN INCREASE IN SHIM PACK WIDTH. SAWDF OVER THE TOP OF
PLYWD & BASE PLATE.

INSULATED GLAZING UNIT, SEE WINDOW SCHEDULE

ALUM. FRAME WINDOW

CONT. BEAD OF SEALANT
OVER BACKER ROD

SELF-ADHERING WINDOW AND
DOOR FLASHING, WRAP AT SILL

22 GA. S.S. SILL PAN AND
REGLET FLASHING

#8 S.S. GASKETED S.M.S. AT
8" O.C.

22 GA. SHT. MET. REMOVABLE
COUNTERFLASHING

S.S. WAFER HEAD ROOFING
SCREWS AT 8" O.C.

20 GA. x 2" WIDE GSM. WIND
CLIPS @ 24" O.C.

TRAFFIC PADS SET IN
ROOFING

MULTIPLE-PLY B.U.R. BASE
FLASHING FEATHERED AT
FIELD OF ROOF

EXTEND FIELD PLIES ABOVE
HEAD OF CANT STRIP

4" FIBER CANT

MULTIPLE-PLY BUILT-UP
ROOFING

3/4" P.T. PLYWOOD
SHEATHING, S.S.D.

3 1/2" RIGID INSULATION

(E) WOOD SHEATHING,
REPAIR AS REQUIRED, V.I.F.

(E) WOOD NAILER BEYOND

4 1/2"   (E) 8" V.I.F.

⚠RFI
609

FIXED SHADE
CLOTH OR
BLACKOUT SHADE
AS SCHEDULED

CONDITION AT
BRACE W.O.
SHOWN DASHED

CONT. BEAD OF
SEALANT

SHADE SPLINE

SHIM AS REQUIRED

CONT. BEAD OF SEALANT
OVER BACKER ROD

ALUM. SHADE FRAME

SPRING CLIP

SHAPED WOOD
CURB FROM
5 1/4"x13 1/2"
GLU-LAM BEAM

ANCHOR CURB
TO (E) STEEL
ANGLES W/(3)
5/8" DIA. STEEL
M.B., NUT AND
WASHERS,
COUNTERSUNK

(E) VERTICAL
STEEL ANGLE AT
TRUSS BEYOND,
V.I.F., TYP.

1/2" GYPSUM
SHEATHING

5 1/4" X 13 1/2"
DEEP GLB WITH
BOTTOM SHAPED TO
SUIT ROOF SLOPE –
see 15/S6.00

SHAPED P.T.
WOOD BLOCKING
FROM 3x4

NOTE: FOR ADDITIONAL DIMS., SEE
1/–; FOR ROOF-CEILING
ASSEMBLY NOTES AND
INFORMATION, SEE 1/A8.51

(4) SECTION: TYP. ROOF AT MONITOR AND SILL AT WINDOW
A8.52 3"=1'-0"

- The "waffle" slab creates substantial areas for the installation of thick insulation within the pans between the two concrete floor surfaces, thus providing a good average R-value over the large area of the exposed building envelope;
- This insulation layer makes it feasible to install a highly energy-efficient radiant heating and cooling floor system, using the new waffle slab for the plastic tubing that carries the heated or chilled water throughout the building; (See *Heating, Ventilating and Cooling Systems, below.*)

XPS rigid-foam insulation is installed within each "waffle" cavity, with the thickness varying from 8" up to a maximum of 14". There is still substantial thermal bridging through the floor beams ("waffle slab" ribs), but the overall R-value for the entire floor, which is exposed to outdoor air conditions beneath the pier, is R-5. The waffle slab is also insulated at the edges with 1" of poly-isocyanurate rigid insulation (R-10) to prevent thermal energy loss at these edges.

Since the floor strengthening was required for the seismic upgrade, this solution was permitted because of the benefits toward the building's goal of ZNE performance. The level of the floor was raised by this system and affected some of the historic details of the column bases (e.g., wheel guards had to be raised to maintain visual proportions at the column base).

The energy efficiency of the structure is limited in part by the lack of a tight seal of the entire building envelope, due principally to the historic preservation requirement that the walls be left to a large degree in their existing condition. The new addition at the end of the pier could be designed at a high level of energy efficiency, however. The new walls are rated at R-19, for example. Standard issues of glare control in the event space plus concerns about "bird strikes" at the clear-glazed surfaces were resolved using modern glass materials with frit patterns, though the glazing area near the observatory space retains clear glazing locally for functional reasons, to ensure good viewing of San Francisco Bay from that location.

Daylighting and Electric Lighting

The tall windows and roof monitors that are part of the original warehouse structure are actually ideal for daylighting the length of the extended building. While the color of the interior surfaces was changed to be neutral rather than the original white throughout, there is nevertheless a good level of daylight penetration to the interior, adequate to provide an ambient level of lighting in the hands-on exhibit areas. Exhibit designers expressed some concern about the amount of daylight that could affect the exhibit spaces, creating conditions of difficult adjustment. The daylight levels are generally a good match with the ambient level desired in the vicinity of the exhibit spaces, however, typically in the range of 0.5 watts/sq.ft.

An effective daylighting design strategy proved to be locating the regular staff office areas on a second-story mezzanine, close to the roof monitors, thus essentially raising the level of daylight available at the work surface level.

The electric light fixtures used for the exhibit areas were selected for their high efficiency. All electric light fixtures are digitally addressable for individual control purposes. There is no dimming of the lights in response to daylight; the primary control is simply on/off and is remotely programmed to scheduled use.

Natural Ventilation

Because of the restrictions on any changes to the historic features of the building, there is little opportunity to introduce design strategies related to natural ventilation for cooling purposes. However, the existing roof ventilators were restored and selected roof monitor windows were replaced with louvers to add relief air. These louvers are tied to a CO_2 sensor and can also be mechanically operated to open when extra ventilation is needed.

View of staff office area on new second floor level, close to daylight from nearby roof monitor (*below and left*).

PHOTO: BRUCE DAMONTE

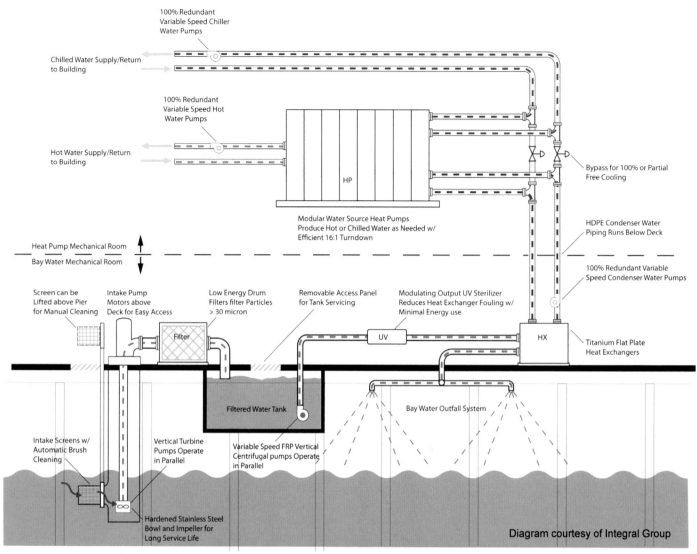

100% Redundant
Variable Speed Chiller
Water Pumps

Chilled Water Supply/Return
to Building

100% Redundant
Variable Speed Hot
Water Pumps

Hot Water Supply/Return
to Building

HP

Modular Water Source Heat Pumps
Produce Hot or Chilled Water as Needed w/
Efficient 16:1 Turndown

Bypass for 100% or Partial
Free Cooling

HDPE Condenser Water
Piping Runs Below Deck

Heat Pump Mechanical Room
Bay Water Mechanical Room

100% Redundant Variable
Speed Condenser Water Pumps

Screen can be
Lifted above Pier
for Manual Cleaning

Intake Pump
Motors above
Deck for Easy Access

Low Energy Drum
Filters filter Particles
> 30 micron

Removable Access Panel
for Tank Servicing

Modulating Output UV Sterilizer
Reduces Heat Exchanger Fouling w/
Minimal Energy use

Filter

UV

HX

Titanium Flat Plate
Heat Exchangers

Filtered Water Tank

Bay Water Outfall System

Intake Screens w/
Automatic Brush
Cleaning

Vertical Turbine
Pumps Operate
in Parallel

Variable Speed FRP Vertical
Centrifugal pumps Operate
in Parallel

Hardened Stainless Steel
Bowl and Impeller for
Long Service Life

Diagram courtesy of Integral Group

(Above) Diagram of original heat pump system design using Bay water below the pier. Vertical turbine pumps were later replaced by submersible pumps located at the bottom of the vertical tubes, after a failure of the vertical turbine pumps at start-up. See discussion on page 129, under *Post Occupancy: HVAC and Commissioning.*

(Right) Heat exchangers (HX) and PVC condenser water piping in Bay water mechanical rooom *(right)*.

PHOTO: BRUCE DAMONTE

Heating, Ventilating and Cooling Systems

With all the historic preservation limitations placed on the standard ZNE design strategies for building envelope, daylighting and natural ventilation, the mechanical system for heating, ventilating and cooling provided the best opportunity for injecting high energy efficiency into the overall design. The ready availability of seawater from San Francisco Bay, in particular, led the design team to consider the use of high efficiency water-source heat pumps to produce heated and chilled water.

In addition, the requirement to strengthen the pier deck, and the decision to create a new concrete floor slab for that purpose, provided another opportunity for even higher efficiency heating and cooling through the use of a radiant floor system. Using the high-efficiency heat pump system to generate the heated or chilled water, a high level of thermal comfort can be maintained at lower temperature setpoints for heating and higher temperature setpoints for cooling compared to air systems, thus lowering energy demand. This is a natural fit of these two types of mechanical system components, which are the basis of the system that was ultimately designed and installed. There were still many challenges for the designers to overcome, however, before these great efficiencies could be realized.

First of all, the cost of this system would clearly be higher than a standard heating and cooling system that would be the alternative, especially considering the special conditions created by the use of seawater and the related maintenance. The design team evaluated life cycle costs for the two approaches and determined that the heat pump system with radiant floors would achieve a payback on the extra investment in 7 to 10 years, including the special design features and expected maintenance costs associated with the use of San Francisco Bay water, compared with the standard boilers, chillers and air systems.

Construction photos showing installation of new structural concrete floor and tubing for radiant heating and cooling system (*above*). *(Photos courtesy of EHDD Architecture)*

The Exploratorium opted for the heat pump approach based on a number of factors in addition to the simple idea that the lease period was much longer than the payback period estimated for the system:

- The space requirement for the central plant equipment is much less for the heat pump system because of higher efficiency of the system and the elimination of any need for a cooling tower;
- Historic preservation restrictions would be triggered by the larger mechanical plant for the standard system, especially since the equipment would have to be located on the pier deck;
- Use of natural gas boilers in the standard system would require additional solar photovoltaic panels to offset the gas energy used (and carbon generated) if the Exploratorium wanted to claim complete ZNE performance, which is a project goal;
- The connection of the building's energy system to the natural environment in the case of the heat pump system is part of the Exploratorium's narrative, consistent with its mission of demonstrating such connections to the public.

Other challenges arose in the design of the system itself, which had to be executed at a very large scale and with great care for its impact on San Francisco Bay in the vicinity of the pier. The system as designed consists of eight 50-ton water-source heat pumps, located in a central plant area. Heat exchangers are required because of the need to separate corrosive seawater from the heat pump equipment; this equipment is actually visible to the public through a display window. (See illustration on opposite page.)

The design and specification of the overall system is similar to that used successfully in nearby public aquarium projects and was well known to the design team. With these designs, the seawater is pumped up into the central plant area where the equipment is in a protected setting that is easily accessible rather than locating the heat exchange coils in the seawater where the equipment is susceptible to wave action and organic deposits.

The seawater temperature averages about 60°F annually, varying 5°F higher or lower with the season. One requirement by the San Francisco Bay Regional Water Quality Control Board is that the seawater must be returned to the Bay within this range of temperature after it is used and must not exceed the highest temperature normally observed. To achieve this, the system introduces some evaporative cooling spray as it is discharged back to the Bay.

Water purity is another closely monitored metric for the seawater, both in the return discharge but also with regard to the seawater being pumped into the system from the Bay. This incoming seawater is filtered for organic material that might affect the equipment operation. There is also a filtration process to prevent small animals, particularly salmon fry, from being drawn into the system. To accomplish this, the design utilizes a type of filter that normally is used on fish farms. The advantage of these filters is that they work primarily by gravity and have a very low pressure drop compared with standard sand filters. The result is a much smaller size and lower energy use for the many pumps that are used in this system, another design choice that lowers the building EUI and contributes to the goal of ZNE performance.

Within the spaces, occupant comfort is maintained using 72 separate thermal zones, some of which may require separate heating or cooling compared to adjacent zones, a normal require-

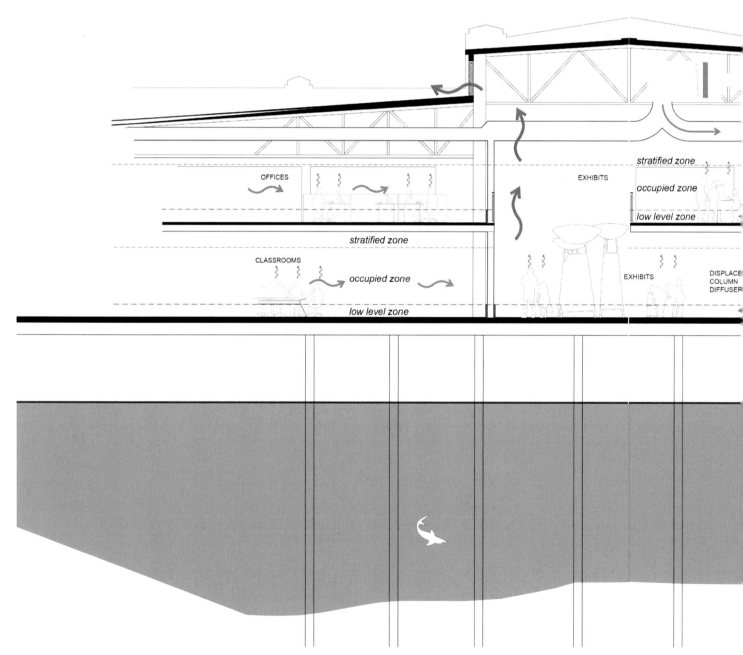

ment in such a large building. The radiant heating or cooling is provided via standard plastic tubing distributed throughout the new floor structure and totaling almost 28 miles of hydronic tubing overall.

Fresh air is brought into the building in four locations, using separate *DOAS* (*dedicated outside air system*) package units. They are *low-velocity, low-pressure drop design*[2]. They are located at floor level to avoid any visual impact on the roof or any reduction in roof area available to the solar PV system. *Displacement ventilation*[3] is also used to increase the overall efficiency of these air-handling units. These units can also function to provide outside air for additional cooling if needed during special peak loads due to high occupancy.

Classrooms, training rooms and conference rooms are additionally equipped with chilled beams to provide extra cooling capacity in those locations.

---

[2] See "Laboratories for the 21st Century: Best Practices, Low-Pressure-Drop HVAC Design for Laboratories", *http://www.nrel.gov/docs/fy05osti/36907.pdf*

[3] *Displacement Ventilation* is a room air distribution method where outside air is supplied at a low velocity near the floor and extracted near the ceiling after the air rises due to it natural buoyancy.

(Below) Diagram of fresh air circulation system using DOAS units and displacement ventilation.

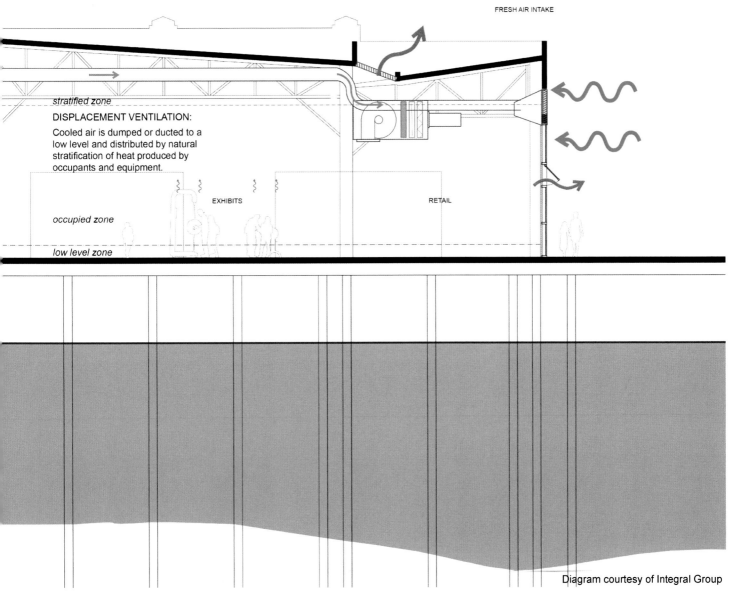

Diagram courtesy of Integral Group

View of some exhibit areas showing local exhibit lighting and low ambient lighting level. *(Below)*

PHOTO: BRUCE DAMONTE

Plug Loads

The plug load evaluation process, which is a mandatory step in any ZNE design process, was carried out in the usual manner: first, all plug loads in the existing building at PFA were carefully measured. These included all electrical energy use created by the equipment designed into the hands-on exhibits. This was followed by an evaluation of the expected expansion created for the new facility, including proposed new exhibits, support space and workshops, which have substantial equipment loads. Finally, the inventory was reviewed for opportunities to reduce these loads through new purchases of energy efficient equipment (*Energy Star*, where applicable).

One of the benefits of the plug load study was the discovery that 33% of the total energy consumed was at night when equipment could ordinarily be shut down. The design team therefore included in the electric power design digitally addressable electric outlets using programmable circuit breakers, allowing control of each equipment item from a central location. By scheduling the power use appropriately, the off-hour plug load is now only 10% of the total.

It should be noted that the two commercial food service establishments, a café and a restaurant, function independently of the Exploratorium. These concessions use natural gas for cooking, which is billed separately by the local utility. Their electric energy is supplied through the Exploratorium system and is billed separately. (Their overall energy use for heating and cooling, however, is included in that of the Exploratorium's total annual energy use, since the radiant floor system is common to the entire building and not separately metered at the tenant spaces.)

Master System Integration and Control Systems

This project was designed in an early period of the development of ZNE building design when the important role of a master system integrator was not well understood. The electrical engineering sub-consultant did not have on staff such a specialized technician and the design team relied to a large degree on control system vendors to provide the expertise. The state-of-art at that time did not include integration of the many control and data monitoring systems that would be required in a ZNE building, especially one as large and complex as the Exploratorium.

The result is the patchwork of control systems typical of that recent period, with no coordination or integration of data monitoring. Energy use is measured via electric power meters that are installed throughout the building, recording data at the panel level in separate categories of space conditioning, lighting and plug loads. This data is sent to a separate *Power and Energy Management System (PEMS)*, which then sends the data on to the main BMS (Building Management System) where it remains uncompiled and unreported.

Energy production is separately recorded at the PV system connection and then at the utility's building meter measuring net electricity flow to and from the power grid. These meter readings for the net energy use for the entire building and the renewable energy production are sent to a dashboard near the building entry for public reporting of the basic level of overall energy use versus overall on-site energy production.

The control system for lighting is completely separate from other systems and is limited to time schedule control only.

The Exploratorium recognizes that the design and operation of the building controls and energy monitoring system are not sufficient for their educational mission, nor for collecting the data necessary to monitor and improve performance over time, and that a greatly improved data recording and reporting system is needed.

Renewable On-Site Energy Supply

5,874 solar photovoltaic panels rated at 245 watts per panel and installed over 80,000 sq. ft. of building roof provide the renewable on-site energy supply. This installation is rated at 1,400 kW (DC), which is approximately 1,250 kW (AC) after inversion. This exceeds the utility's net metering limit of 1,000 kW (AC) by 250 kW (AC). The Exploratorium uses the separately circuited 250 kW (AC) directly on-site without any storage and relies on the connection of the remaining 1,000 kW (AC) to the utility for net metering operation.

Once the design had been scoped out and modeled, analysis indicated that the building roof provided enough area suitable for good solar exposure for the solar panels to generate sufficient energy to offset the building's demand, achieving the ZNE performance goal. However, a number of factors led to a reduction in the number of panels allowed, a change in their optimum tilt angle and in their production performance.

- The large roof monitor that provides daylight to the interior along the entire length of the building also shades a substantial area on one side of the roof adjacent to the monitor.

PHOTO: AMY SNYDER
©EXPLORATORIUM

• While some limitations on the solar panels by the historic preservation agencies was expected, the nearby *Telegraph Hill Neighborhood Association* insisted that the solar photovoltaic panels be installed flat to the existing roof to minimize visual impact to the neighborhood, which is located a half-mile away.

• This in turn led to a major problem with the local sea bird population, who were attracted to the flat panel surfaces for nesting and perching. The result is an excessive amount of bird guano on the panels, severely affecting their performance. "Bird-safe" solutions are being tried but the Exploratorium has nevertheless committed to a much more intensive maintenance and cleaning program for the solar panels.

PHOTO: AMY SNYDER
©EXPLORATORIUM

The net result of these impacts is that there is no margin for sub-ZNE performance due to weather (or extra bird activity). The Exploratorium considered using the roof of Pier 17 for additional PV panels serving both piers to provide some energy production margin, but the roof strengthening requirements for this ancillary building were deemed to be too expensive. The renewable energy supply for the Pier 15 building is therefore limited to the current installation. See *Energy Production versus Energy Use: Zero Net Energy*, below, for actual ZNE performance measurements for the first two years of occupancy.

PHOTO: AMY SNYDER
©EXPLORATORIUM

Energy Design Analysis and Energy Performance:
Modeling versus Post-Occupancy Measurements

Energy Use — Modeling

Energy modeling was carried out during the design phases using *eQuest v3.65*. The modeling analysis showed a total energy use of 2,668 MWh per year, or an EUI of 47.2 kBtu/sq.ft per year. The much larger building (approximately 200,000 sq. ft.) with its limited access to daylighting and the added energy loads for a building of this type are the reasons for the larger EUI compared to the other case study buildings in this Volume 2[4]. As a reference point, the ASHRAE 90.1 2007 baseline EUI was calculated to be 81.3, so the Exploratorium's modeled energy performance is more than 40% lower than the recommended ASHRAE benchmark.

Energy Use — Actual Measurement and Comparison to Modeling Results

Since there was no master system integrator included on the project team, there is currently no integration of energy use data monitoring for the different energy subsystems and there is no design of the metering system to ensure that data recording is in place appropriate to type of energy use. As noted above in the section, *Master System Integration and Control Systems*, data from power meters installed at each panel is sent to the BMS via a PEMS. Data extraction from the BMS is difficult and time-consuming and there is no design for real-time reporting to a user interface. Trending information is therefore simply not available. Furthermore, these power meters at the panels may have some inaccuracies since power meters frequently drift and need regular checking.

The building's energy use as measured by the power meter system has proven to be off by some margin—30% over the first two years of building occupancy—when compared with the utility's main building meter at the power grid boundary. The latter is reliably accurate, recording the total net metered electric energy flows. The shortfall of the energy use recorded at the building's electric panels is likely due to a number of contributing factors, including errors in extracting the data from the BMS, some meters not programmed into the system, missed electric panels upstream of the meters, as well as meter inaccuracies that have yet to be determined.

The engineering team believes that the data recorded at the building's electric panels accurately reflect the *percentage* of total energy use attributable to each category, namely the lighting, plug load and "mechanical" (that is, heating, cooling, pump and fan energy use) on a monthly basis and for the entire year. As with earlier case study buildings, separate metering for heating and cooling operation was not specified with the heat pump system. Thus the measurement data shows only the combined "mechanical" category.

The methodology used to produce the accompanying charts showing measured energy use by category is therefore to apply these percentages to the total building energy use as measured by the utility meter.

The general trend over the first two years (2014-2015) is that the energy use by the building is constant every month, which is due simply to the small variation in exterior conditions over the course of the year and the fairly constant exhibit lighting loads and plug loads. As can be seen from the annual pie charts and monthly bar charts, there is close correlation of the actual measured energy use with the whole building energy modeling results for 2015. 2014 had similar performance results, though the building was still in its tune-up period. The measured annual energy use in 2015 was 2,461 MWh, or an EUI equal to 43.5 kBtu/sq.ft. per year. (Domestic hot water use was not measured separately and is included in the "Mechanical" category of energy use.)

---

[4] Note: the floor area of the tenant space is <u>not</u> included in the EUI calculation except as noted in the chart on the opposite page.

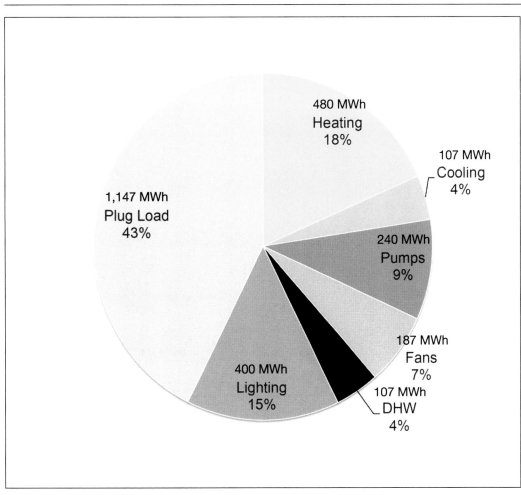

Modeled Energy Use
(Annual)

2,668 MWh/year
Modeled EUI = 47.2

(1 MWh = 1,000 kWh)

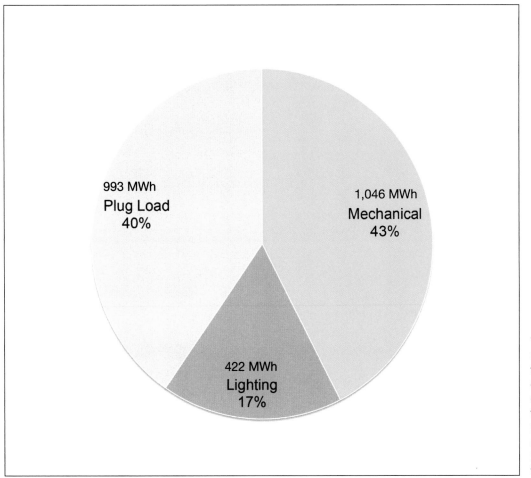

Measured Energy Use
(2015)

2,461 MWh/year
Measured EUI = 43.5

"Mechanical" =
Heating*, Cooling*, Pumps,
Fans and DHW

*Heating and cooling energy used in the restaurant and café tenant space is included in this energy use category ("Mechanical"). Energy used in these tenant spaces in other categories is separately metered and excluded. Tenant floor area is not included in the EUI calculation.

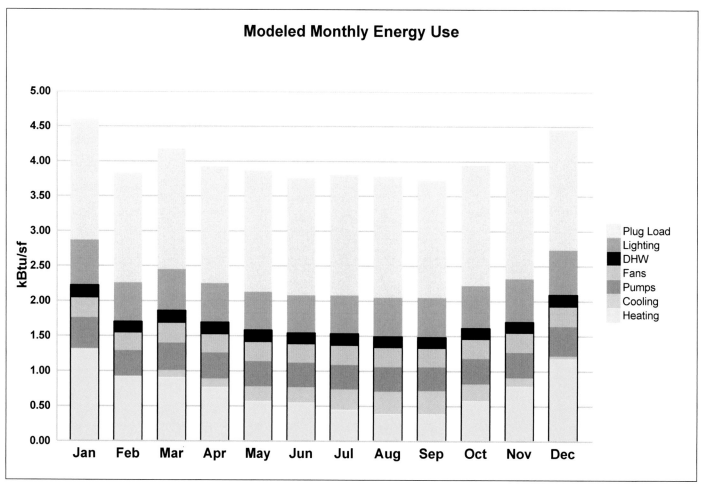

Modeled Monthly Energy Use

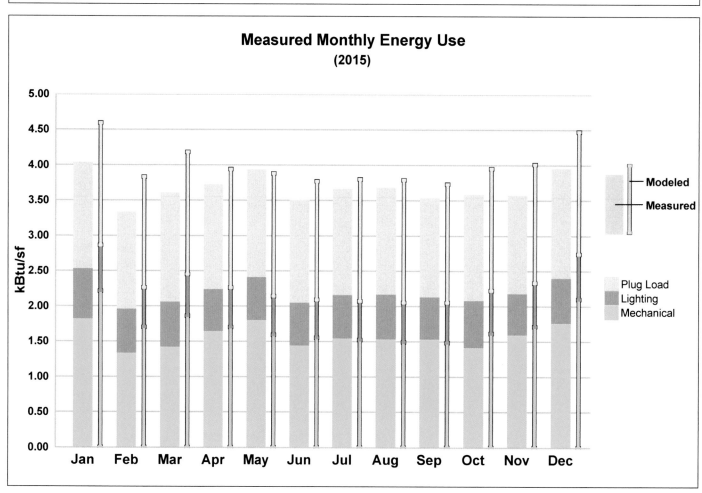

Measured Monthly Energy Use
(2015)

Energy Production versus Energy Use — Zero Net Energy Performance

The energy production by the solar PV system is separately and accurately recorded as part of that system's operation. Using the utility meter data, the standard charts can be constructed showing the building energy use versus the on-site production and the cumulative net energy performance over the two year period. These measured data show that the building has been performing below the ZNE goal, with total annual on-site energy production at 83% of the total annual energy use, not the 100%+ needed to make it a ZNE-performing building.

Since the building is using an amount of energy slightly less than that determined from the energy modeling, the issue appears to be simply an under-production by the solar photovoltaic system. While the number of panels was originally expected to be adequate to offset the design loads, adjustments to the panel layout and unexpected maintenance issues appear to have lowered the production below the desired threshold. The PV panel performance was severely hampered by the presence of sea birds, as noted above.

Combined with a greatly enhanced solar PV panel cleaning schedule, the Exploratorium's program to reduce plug loads and engage staff for further reductions in energy use should help to bring into balance the two curves of Energy Use and Energy Production, resulting in an annual ZNE performance. Though a less likely scenario, changing out some of the original PV panels for replacements with higher production would also raise the production level and bring the building to a net positive performance level.

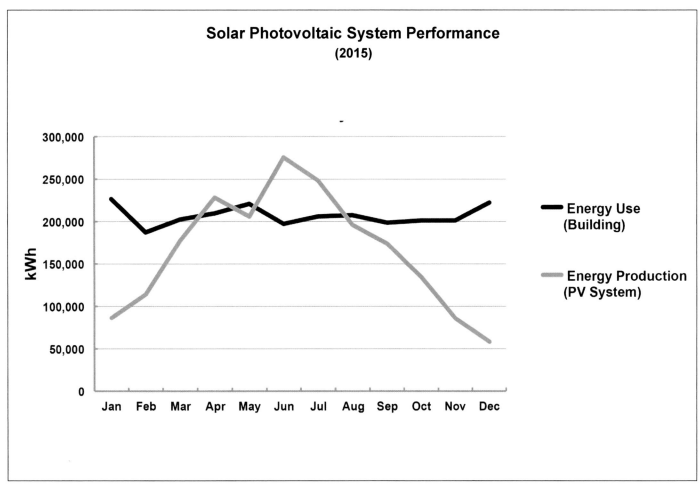

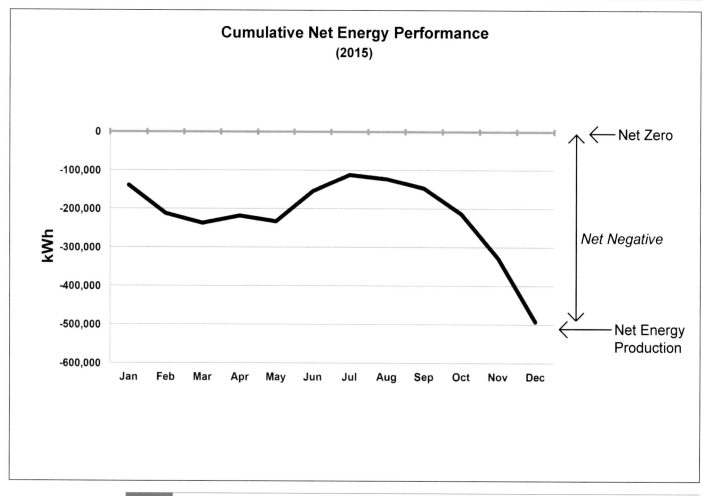

Post Occupancy: Observations and Conclusions

As might be imagined, moving and setting up operations at the new, larger facility involved a prodigious effort on the part of the Exploratorium staff and required some time to make everything functional and ready for the public. Commissioning such a large and complex building was equally as challenging, particularly considering the unusual nature of some of the building systems. Much of the post-occupancy period since the building opening in 2013 has been taken up by these tasks and most of the post-occupancy issues are the result of the transition to the new facility and the startup of its unconventional systems.

Some issues, however, are actually common issues for properly "tuned" ZNE buildings, as noted in the earlier case study buildings, and are discussed below.

Post Occupancy: Controls and Monitoring

One common issue affecting the ZNE performance is the missing integration of the control systems and energy monitoring systems. With no design for this during the planning and design phases of the project, the opportunity to monitor and improve the building's energy performance is limited. At times, there are problems that arise which have an adverse effect and are simply undetected. An example of the latter is a software update for a control system that overrode some equipment schedules and the DOAS fans ran all night for three months before anyone noticed.

One of the principal problems remains the onerous task of extracting measurement data from the BMS. In the absence of the master system integrator from the design team, a metering design program was not done. That is, there was no design for establishing which meters together comprised measurement for a specific category of energy use.

The net result is that the Exploratorium is currently not able to monitor the performance of the energy system components on a regular basis—a major data extraction effort is required—and there is no breakdown of the energy use by category readily available (heating, cooling, lighting, plug load) so that progress toward the ZNE goal can be tracked.

PHOTO: BRUCE DAMONTE

The Exploratorium recognizes that the controls and monitoring systems need an integrative overhaul and must include the data monitoring system so that energy use trending can be readily observed and tracked in all pertinent categories. Once this is completed, a truly informative *energy dashboard* for public education purposes can be programmed to provide the real-time environmental story of the facility itself. It is the latter opportunity that motivates the Exploratorium to make this systems overhaul a high priority now that the move-in period is coming to an end.

Post Occupancy: HVAC and Commissioning

As noted, the complexity and uniqueness of the HVAC system posed challenges during the early post-occupancy period, which were met during the commissioning period. Some of these challenges were of the standard type, others were not.

An example of the unexpected challenge is the initial failure of the vertical turbine pumps used to pump the seawater from San Francisco Bay up to the heat exchange equipment at pier deck level. These industrial-grade inline pumps were placed at the top of the vertical tubes that extend below the pier into the water. Similar to the design at the Seattle Aquarium, this type of installation allows ready access to the pumps for maintenance above the water. In the case of the Exploratorium plant, however, the turbine bearings burned out immediately on start-up. This has been attributed to the length of tube segments required at this installation and the unfortunate resonance of these segments with the pump motor vibration. This amplified the vibrating motion and, combined with the unexpectedly corrosive conditions of the relatively still water in the Bay, caused the bearings to fail.

The design was changed to submersible pumps located at the bottom of the vertical tubes. The submersible pumps are standard equipment and can be serviced by the Exploratorium staff using a winch system to allow for monthly maintenance and inspection. The industrial-grade vertical turbine pumps required outside specialists for maintenance. The final solution is actually more suitable to the Exploratorium's general "hands-on" approach to design and problem-solving.

Beyond the start-up and commissioning issues, both small and large, the operation of the unconventional HVAC system has been relatively trouble-free.

Post Occupancy: Lighting

The very low level of ambient lighting as designed to supplement the exhibit lighting, namely 0.5 watts per sq. ft., is working well and has contributed to the low overall lighting energy use. The building staff would prefer a more robust lighting control system, however, that has more flexibility in the time controls and could respond to daylight conditions.

Post Occupancy: Occupant Behavior

One noticeable (but predictable) occupant response to a ZNE design feature occurred at the staff office space, which is set on a second level within the high volume of the building. This location raised the office area close to the roof monitor, where direct sunlight can penetrate and create a severe glare problem at computers and general work surfaces.

In general, however, the Exploratorium staff are very conscious of the ZNE performance goal for the building and have responded accordingly. Since the performance over the 2014-2015 settling-in period has fallen short of this goal, though improving over time, the staff are focusing more on behaviors and system adjustments to bring the building to that level of performance.

Conclusion ▷

Observations

The case study buildings documented and discussed in this Volume 2 represent a certain advance in understanding of the design strategies and building technologies that produce the best performance results for ZNE buildings. This has come about as a result of communication of the results and experience with early ZNE buildings as well as the appearance of new technologies that have been recently developed to improve operation and general performance. At the end of Volume 1 of *Zero Net Energy Case Study Buildings*, the section on *Observations* took note of some common issues with the early ZNE building projects documented there. It's interesting to compare those observations with similar aspects of the case study buildings in Volume 2, confirming the advance in understanding and resolution of some of those issues.

Energy Modeling versus Actual Performance

Generally, the same observations apply about whole building energy modeling being used to set energy performance targets or predict results—there are limitations and design professionals cannot guarantee a certain level of performance during the first years of occupancy. Comparing the energy modeling results with the measured performance for the buildings in Volume 2, the actual energy use tracks the modeling data well, with some expected variation due to the drought-year weather and clear skies experienced by most of these buildings when the full-year measurements were done.

Building Metering and Monitoring Issues

For all of the projects in Volume 1, the metering and energy monitoring systems essentially had to be commissioned and required post-occupancy adjustments to function properly. For the two projects where the accuracy of the metering system was in fact tested by comparing its results with the utility meter, the building metering system had to be overhauled to ensure reliable results going forward.

While this assessment of the quality of the data being recorded is still required, the case study buildings in Volume 2 that incorporated a master control system were also connected to an online dashboard for easy energy data reporting and review. Extracting and communicating data from the different building systems is relatively straightforward when the metering/monitoring system is part of the overall integrated controls and communication system. Given the importance of making energy use data "actionable" in order to optimize building performance, the installation of a master control system, as demonstrated by several of the case study buildings, facilitates this purpose.

Integrated Master Control Systems

The case study buildings of Volume 2 demonstrate at least one significant advance in the design of ZNE buildings, namely, the value of the master control system and the new corresponding design team role of systems integrator. This is discussed in some detail in the Introduction, as well as in each of the case studies. Suffice it to say that this particular new development in building technology and systems design will become part of the best practices for design of ZNE buildings.

Acknowledgments

The following individuals—clients, designers, contractors, commissioning agents and remarkably skilled technicians—are owed a great deal of thanks for giving their valuable time in lengthy interviews and sharing an amazing amount of valuable information that accurately and thoroughly describes the story of their projects. Thanks also for their patience with the many follow-up emails and phone calls about design details, their extra work confirming performance data and their time reviewing the draft case study for completeness and accuracy. Without this openness and supportive effort, the case studies would be quite incomplete and not nearly as valuable as they are proving to be.

Special thanks to Margaret Pigman of Resource Refocus for the thorough review of each case study and for the development of the comparison charts for modeled performance versus measured performance, and to Can Anbarlilar of PG&E for equally thorough review.

Also to the following key clients and client representatives for spending their valuable time describing the entire process from concept through operation and, in particular, how design decisions were made along the way. The generosity with their time, especially for the subsequent telephone conversations and communications about project details, was exceptional.

Kevin Bates, Partner, Sharp Development Co., Inc.

Byron Benton, Training Director, Joint Apprenticeship Training Committee, IBEW-NECA

Shani Krevsky, Project Director, Exploratorium Campus

Ted van der Linden, Director of Sustainability, DPR Construction

The following design team members gave time for interviews, provided an enormous amount of information, including drawings, diagrams and other images, and made themselves available to answer the many inevitable follow-up questions:

John Andary, Principal, Integral Group

Shannon Allison, Integral Group

Michael Bulander, Harley Ellis Devereaux Architects

Dylan Connelly, Integral Group

Jeff Dittman, Belden Engineers

Galen Grant, Principal, FCGA Architects

Jennifer Harding, Fee Munson Ebert Architects

Michael Hummel, Sustainability Consultant, EBS Consultants Inc.

Marc L'Italien, Principal, EHDD Architecture

David Kaneda, Managing Principal, Integral Group

Gerard Lee, Harley Ellis Devereaux Architects

Tara Ogle, Architect, EHDD Architecture

Steven Stenton, Principal, RMW Architects

Joseph Wenisch, Associate Principal, Integral Group

A special thank-you is owed to the *master system integrators* who played key roles in a number of the case study buildings and who spent time sharing their knowledge of this emerging field of expertise.

Robert Wallace, Building Controls Engineer, Energy Etc

Joell Morris, Controls Tech, Trinity EMCS

Eric Sande, Owner, Intertie Automation

Max Parfet, Controls Tech, Honeywell

Another special thank-you to Chris Buntine, Technical Leader, Built Environment Sustainability, Aurecon, who spent time specifically for this case study publication re-constructing his energy model that was used in the design phases of the West Berkeley Branch Library (Case Study No. 10).

Thanks to Neal DeSnoo, Energy Program Officer (Office of Energy and Sustainable Development, City of Berkeley Planning Department) for providing the energy performance data for the West Berkeley Branch Library as well as information about post-occupancy operation of the building.

Thanks to Alex Krickx of Integral Group, who reviewed the energy metering system diagram for the Speculative Office Building at 435 Indio Way (Case Study No. 9) and energy data report for the entire subject year, successfully confirming the accuracy of the energy-use reported per category of use.

I would like to thank the professionals who provided valuable additional information and reference documents for the case study buildings, invaluable for this publication:

Orry Nottingham, P.E., CAP, Commissioning Agent

Max Pierson, Miniscule Lighting Design

Lindsey Gaunt, Integral Group

Robert Boyd, Principal, Cammisa + Wipf Consulting Engineers

Finally, continuing thanks for supporting the idea of this series about *Zero Net Energy Case Study Buildings* to Peter Turnbull, Principal, Commercial Buildings, Pacific Gas and Electric Company, and Anna LaRue, Principal, Resource Refocus LLC.

--Edward Dean, FAIA, Bernheim + Dean, Inc.

52323750R00088

Made in the USA
Lexington, KY
11 September 2019